Fourth C
Languag

Reading Book 1
Lessons 1 to 50

Visit **McRuffy.com** for helpful resources to teach this curriculum!

Reading Book 1
ISBN 978159269-1593

McRuffy Press Fourth Grade Language Arts Curriculum
ISBN 978159269-1555

Written and illustrated by
Brian Davis M. A. Ed.

Graphic Design by
Sherylynn Davis

McRuffy Press, LLC
P.O. Box 212
Raymore, MO 64083

816-331-7831

sales@mcruffy.com

www.McRuffy.com

Book 1 Table of Contents

Matthew and the Sizzle Saucer

Story by Brian Davis

Illustrations based on drawings by Ron Wheeler

Matthew and the Sizzle Saucer

A small disc brings big challenges for Matthew Day as he learns to toss away fear, jealousy, envy, and even a Sizzle Saucer!

Chapter		Page

Vocabulary Words

avalanche
celebrities
certificate
commercial
concession
illegally
impersonating
predicted
sheepishly
sponsoring

Chapter 1

Officer Trouble

Matthew Day stared at the sleek red mountain bike inside the sporting goods store window. Suddenly, a dark shadow moved up behind him. Matthew thought a cloud had blocked the sun.

"It's almost big enough for me," chuckled Nathan. "Just needs some super heavy duty shocks!"

Nathan Goliath was the biggest nine-year-old that Matthew had ever seen. Most people would have thought he was a big bully the first time they saw him. Well, maybe not most people, but Matthew did. It turned out that Nathan wasn't such a bad guy after all. But, that's a whole different story.

Matthew almost fell over as the large hand patted him on the back. Matthew wasn't quite used to having a friend like Nathan Goliath. The large boy made Matthew feel so small in comparison. Still, he figured it's better to have big friends than big enemies.

"Are you going to buy it?" asked Nathan.

"Yes," sighed Matthew, "but only in my dreams. I'm okay with my old bike. Besides, I only have five dollars."

"That's not enough for a sleek red mountain bike," Nathan sighed. Then he pointed to something inside the store. "But it might be just enough for that!"

The large boy rushed to the doorway. Matthew wondered what the excitement was all about. Nathan bumped a police officer who was writing a parking ticket on a car. The officer dropped the tablet he was writing on.

Matthew could almost predict what would happen next, but was too slow (or too amused) to stop it. A man carrying a fishing pole tried to leave the store. Nathan tried to squeeze by him. The two shoppers danced around each other. Finally, Nathan rushed by, sending the man into an unbalanced spin.

The pole swung around and struck the police officer who was still bent over. The fishing pole made a loud smacking sound right on the seat of the police officer's pants. Needless to say, the officer was not very pleased. The man with the pole sheepishly hid it behind his back. Of course, the top of the pole was plain to see over the man's head.

"The boy pushed me into you," the fisherman tried to explain.

The officer looked at Matthew. Matthew gulped and turned a little pale. The officer's eyebrows got all crinkled as he stared at Matthew. "Young man, do you have an explanation for this? Knocking me over, and then pushing this man into me?"

"I…uh…," Matthew was usually good at thinking of something in a crisis. Lots of times the things he thought of weren't all that useful, or even helpful. Yet, he normally thought of something. This time, he was speechless.

"Not him," explained the man with the fishing pole. "It was a big boy, huge. I think he went that way." The man pointed down the street. "Don't move from here. I'll be right back!" said the officer as he trotted down the street.

"Tell your friend to be more careful in the future!" the man with the fishing pole warned Matthew as soon as the policeman was out of sight.

Suddenly the fisherman wasn't so sheepish. Matthew wondered why the man told the officer a lie. Soon, he knew the answer. The man hurriedly stuffed the fishing pole into the back of his car. It was the same car the officer had been ticketing. It was illegally parked.

Then the man reached for something under the car.

It was the police officer's ticket book. "No copies, no ticket!" smiled the man as he tore out some pages from the tablet the officer had dropped.

Matthew watched as the man with the fishing pole sped away in his car. Matthew wasn't sure if he had witnessed a crime or not. He really didn't want to stick around for the angry police officer to come back. He rushed into the store. Matthew ducked behind the mountain bike and watched through the window.

Within seconds, the policeman returned. He spun around in all directions obviously looking for anyone involved in the fishing pole incident. Then he spied his ticket book on the sidewalk. The officer bent over to pick it up.

At that moment, another man left the sporting goods store carrying a pair of water skis. Just then a car honked. Someone shouted out the man's name. The man with the skis turned around. Smack! The skis struck the bent over officer right on the seat of the pants.

The officer dropped the ticket book to catch his fall. He stood up and shook his finger in the face of the man with the skis. Matthew couldn't hear what the police officer was saying. It was probably a good thing. There are some words young boys shouldn't hear.

Suddenly the officer froze. He slowly turned around. A street sweeper was coming up the street. The two large brushes kicked up a little dust as they vacuumed every small object in their path.

The driver of the rumbling machine made a special effort to steer into the empty space on the street in front of the sporting goods store. There was a pad of paper cluttering the gutter. The officer's face dropped. Before he could move, the machine hungrily gobbled up the police officer's ticket book.

An avalanche of bouncing ping pong balls turned Matthew's attention away from the scene on the sidewalk. "Sorry," he heard Nathan's friendly voice somewhere in the store. Matthew began scooping up the balls. He was soon joined by other customers who worked their way back to the ping pong ball display to dump their loads.

"I need your five dollars," said Nathan.

"What for?" asked Matthew, "Ping pong balls?"

"No, I'll show you," said Nathan as he pointed to the front of the store.

Just then, a jingling bell rang above the door of the store. A very angry policeman was tromping down the aisle.

"Don't move from here," the policeman's words echoed in Matthew's mind.

"I've got to go," said Matthew nervously as he ducked behind a shelf.

"The money?" pleaded Nathan.

Matthew reached in his pocket and handed Nathan the five dollar bill. Matthew normally didn't like to loan money. It usually turned out a lot like giving away money. This time it worked to his advantage. Nathan took the money and immediately ran into the police officer. The officer stumbled backwards and fell right into a display of tennis balls. Matthew swiftly made his escape from the store without the policeman ever noticing.

Chapter 2

Our **Sizzle Saucer**

The next day…

With blazing speed, Matthew Day zipped by the cheetah on his right. He had passed the fastest animal on land. The boy stretched out his chest to cross the finish line. Then, it happened. Matthew fell flat on his face. The cheetah stopped to lick Matthew's nose.

There was something strange about the cheetah. It had doggie breath. It also had a doggie tongue and teeth. In fact, the cheetah looked just like Buster, his pup.

"Are you okay?" asked Nathan Goliath.

Matthew groaned. Wherever Nathan Goliath was, disaster wasn't too far behind.

"What happened?" asked Matthew as he lay on the grass of the park.

"You were running with Buster, and you fell," said Nathan. "I tried to warn you, but you weren't listening."

"I was pretending I was in a Double-Pump Slammer commercial. I was just about to the part where I out-run a cheetah."

"You do know that cheetahs can run over sixty miles per hour, don't you?" asked Nathan. "I mean, not even Double-Pump Slammers can make you run that fast. No shoes could do that, unless they had jet packs on them or something. I think jet packs would be pretty hard on your ankles. They would get really hot. They would probably set your socks on fire."

"I know," sighed Matthew. "But, I can outrun Buster. He makes a pretty good pretend cheetah, except for the doggie breath."

"Well, I'm sorry I made you trip," said Nathan.

"You tripped me?" asked Matthew.

Nathan picked up a red plastic disc about the size and shape of a dinner plate. It was at Matthew's feet.

"This made you trip," explained Nathan. "It's my new Sizzle Saucer. Or, should I say *our* Sizzle Saucer?"

"*Our* Sizzle Saucer?" asked Matthew."Fifty-fifty. Or rather, five hundred, five hundred, cents that is. Your five dollars and my five dollars were just enough to purchase this fine flying disc for the both of us. You can use it one week. I can use it the next. Or we could switch every other day, or even better we can play together!"

Matthew rubbed his leg, "That's wonderful," he replied with a frown. Nathan didn't detect the lack of joy in Matthew's voice.

Matthew wasn't thrilled about co-owning anything with Nathan Goliath. They were barely friends. "Going halvesies" on a saucer wasn't exactly the way he had planned to spend the money. More importantly, tossing a piece of plastic around with Nathan Goliath wasn't exactly the way Matthew planned to spend all his free time.

"It can really fly. You ran right into its path," Nathan tried to explain. "I'm sorry I didn't see you coming. You are a pretty fast runner."

"Well, try to be more careful next time," said Matthew as he stood to his feet and brushed off his clothes.

"Hey, just to make it up to you, I'll teach you my new trick," smiled Nathan.

He handed the Sizzle Saucer to Matthew. "Toss it right above my head."

"Are you sure you want me throwing at your head?" said Matthew. "Remember the first time I pitched to you in a baseball game. Do you *want* another headache?"

"I trust you," said Nathan. "But, don't throw it right at my head. Throw it here."

Nathan pointed to a spot a few inches to the left of his head. Matthew gripped the saucer. He spun around and let go. The Sizzle Saucer hit the ground and rolled in a circle. It bumped into Buster. The pup jumped.

"I think it's a Fizzle Saucer when I throw it," sighed Matthew.

"I think we need to start from the beginning," laughed Nathan.

Nathan taught Matthew how to throw the Sizzle Saucer that afternoon. Well, Matthew sort of learned how to throw the flying disc. He hadn't quite mastered it, but Matthew was sure with a little practice he would be just as good as Nathan. The two boys enjoyed playing. Even Buster liked catching the saucer.

"Now if we can just teach him to throw," said Matthew.

"It's possible. I taught you," teased Nathan. "Anyway, we have two weeks to practice."

"Two weeks?" Matthew was almost afraid to ask.

"Until the big saucer contest," explained Nathan. "We're both entered. It's the big event at the Hometown Days Festival. They even named it after you, Hometown *Days*, Matthew *Day*."

Matthew groaned, "Why would you enter *us* into a contest?"

"You helped pay for the Sizzle Saucer," said Nathan. "Buy a Sizzle Saucer and get a free entry into the contest. The sporting goods store is sponsoring it."

"Sponsoring?"

"You know. They're the ones giving away the prizes," answered Nathan.

"Is first prize a sleek red mountain bike?" asked Matthew hopefully.

"Better," said Nathan. "First prize is new pair of Double-Pump Slammers, your favorite shoes. You know. It's the Sky Bordon ones with the blue soles."

Matthew sighed, "What's second prize?" Sky Bordon wasn't at the top of the list of his favorite basketball players any more.

"There are all kinds of prizes and gift certificates," explained Nathan. "We could even win another Sizzle Saucer! All we have to do is come up with the best tricks."

"Can't you find someone else?" hesitated Matthew.

A sad puppy dog look came on Nathan's face. Matthew knew the look. It was the same expression on Buster's face. The large boy was holding the small dog and gently petting its head. It was the saddest thing Matthew had ever seen.

"Ok," Matthew caved in.

"Yahoo partner!" shouted Nathan. He began chattering excitedly, "Now if we win the shoes how should we do this? You wear them one week. I'll wear them the next. Or would you rather switch every other day?"

"If they fit you," Matthew explained, "You could wear them in the summer. I could use them as snow skis in the winter." Nathan looked at his feet, "That just might work!"

Chapter 3

Tricks, But No Treats

There was a carnival atmosphere in the park. The Hometown Days Festival was filled with contests and events. Game booths were set up and children were standing in line to play. There were bake sales and food stands. The smell of cooking oil and barbecue smoke filled the air. The most popular attraction was the dunking booth. People waited in line to throw baseballs at a target that would drop town celebrities into a large water tank.

"Where is he?" asked Rail as he tossed Matthew the red Sizzle Saucer.

Rail was Matthew's best friend. He was the opposite of Nathan. Rail was the smallest, thinnest nine-year-old in school. That's why everyone called him Rail. He was as thin as a rail.

"If Nathan was here, we would surely see him," Matthew looked over the crowd that had gathered in the park for the flying disc contest. He didn't notice any giant nine-year-olds. There were no sounds of anything breaking. The park appeared to be a Nathan-free zone. For once, that's what worried him.

Nathan and Matthew were a team. Actually, Matthew hadn't quite mastered the Sizzle Saucer. He basically helped Nathan do the tricks by tossing him the disc. Matthew didn't expect Nathan to be late for the contest. He was getting more worried as he tossed the disc to Rail. Matthew wasn't concentrating on his throws.

The Sizzle Saucer soared wildly over Rail's head and into a crowd. Someone yelled, "Duck!" All but one person managed to get out of the way. The disc smacked right into the policeman's hat. The brim of the hat blocked his view long enough for him to fall right into the dunking booth.

Matthew had followed the disc into the crowd. He picked up the Sizzle Saucer. His jaw dropped when he saw who had fallen into the tank. It was the same officer from the sporting goods store. Matthew quickly got lost in the crowd.

"Please gather around the baseball field for the flying disc contest," spoke a voice over a loud speaker.

"The contest is about to start," said Matthew's mother as she rushed up to him.

"Where's Nathan?" asked his dad. Matthew shrugged his shoulders.

"I have Buster," said Rachel, Matthew's older sister, as she walked up to him. The dog was on a leash and seemed very anxious to explore all the dropped food around the concession stands. She handed the leash to her brother.

Matthew got at the end of the line of contestants. He wanted to give Nathan as much time as possible. Matthew watched team after team do all kinds of tricks with flying discs. He was getting very nervous as he waited.

"Next up is Nathan, Matthew, and Buster the wonder pup!" said the announcer.

Matthew led Buster to the center of the baseball diamond. He unhooked the leash from the pup's collar. Matthew looked helplessly at the fans in the stands. His mother was waving at him. Where was Nathan? Matthew didn't know what to do.

"This could be fun. Can we boo him?" Rachel asked her mom.

"We've got to help him," Mrs. Day tugged her husband's arm.

"We're going to walk out there and do what? Embarrass him more?" sighed Mr. Day.

As Rail stood by the fence somebody walked by a trash can and threw away some paper cups. That gave him an idea. He dug through the trash and found three lightly used plates. The thin boy ran onto the field.

Rail tossed the plates in the air, one, two, and three. He was juggling them as he joined Matthew in the center of the baseball diamond. Rail tossed them higher and higher. The crowd began to cheer.

Rail finished the juggling by catching all three plates behind his back. Matthew was shocked. He never knew Rail had such hidden talent.

"A spectacular juggling demonstration by Nathan!" said the announcer.

Rail had to giggle. The small boy never imagined someone would mistake him for the giant Nathan Goliath. He took a small bow. Next, he turned and waved toward Matthew.

A confused look was on Matthew's face. He wasn't sure why Rail waved. He took a deep breath. A voice in his head said, "Do something." The crowd began to clap in rhythm.

Matthew gripped the Sizzle Saucer in his hand. He threw it as high in the air as he could. He was preparing to catch it behind his back. That's when he noticed the police officer.

He seemed to have recognized Matthew and was trotting onto the baseball diamond.

The officer was moving right into the path of the saucer. Matthew couldn't watch. He closed his eyes. Just then, he heard a whistle. Rail was calling Buster.

Rail bent low to the ground. The pup leaped onto the small boy's back. Rail timed it just right and sprung into the air. The pup flew to the saucer, caught it in its teeth. The pup then did a flip and landed right in the policeman's arms. The crowd jumped to their feet in applause.

The policeman waved to the crowd. Buster licked his face. Rail took another bow. He turned again to Matthew. There was an empty space where Matthew had been standing.

From behind the stands Matthew listened to the applause. Everyone was having a great time, except him.

"Are you ready?" came a voice from the line at the concession stands.

"Nathan! Where have you been?" asked Matthew.

"I've been getting ready for the contest," answered Nathan. "A little snack always calms me down."

"The contest is over," said Matthew.

"What do you mean over? It doesn't begin until two o'clock," Nathan pulled a flier from his pocket and handed it to Matthew.

Matthew looked at the paper.

"Were you eating cake when you picked up this flier?" asked Matthew.

"Wow, are you like a detective or something? How did you know?" asked Nathan.

"There is some white icing on it," he scratched the food off the flier. "It says 12:00. The icing covered up the one."

"Oops, I guess I should have used a napkin," grinned Nathan. "Did we win?"

Chapter 4

On the Lam

"You missed the awards ceremony," said Mrs. Day when she came through the front door.

Matthew was waiting for his parents on the couch. He had something to tell them.

"Mom, Dad, I have to let you know, I'm a wanted boy," said Matthew.

"Of course you are," said his mom. "We all want you around here."

"Maybe not *all* of us," said Rachel.

"Quiet Rachel," said her dad. "Can't you see your brother needs a little encouragement?"

"I do give him little encouragement," Rachel defended herself.

"You don't understand," interrupted Matthew. "I'm wanted by the police. I'm on the lam."

"On the lam?" laughed Mr. Day. "Where did you hear that phrase?"

"On an old gangster movie," answered Matthew.

"You're wanted by the police for what?" asked his mom.

"For impersonating a saucer thrower," giggled Rachel.

"For attacking a police officer," Matthew tried to explain.

His parents looked shocked and all of the sudden a bit worried.

"I didn't actually attack the officer. Nathan did." Matthew's parents looked even more concerned. "He didn't mean to. He just bumped into him in front of the sporting goods store a few weeks ago. But, the policeman thought I did it. I was just a scapegoat."

His parents looked more relieved.

"So, you've been on the lam ever since," concluded his dad with a little smile.

"It's not funny, Dad," said Matthew. "The police officer at the contest was after me. I don't want to get Nathan in trouble and I don't want to go to the big house."

"Big house?" asked his mom.

"Prison," explained Mr. Day. "I saw the same gangster movie."

"Then, I witnessed a crime," Matthew added. "I saw a man who bought a fishing pole tear up a parking ticket."

Matthew heard a siren outside, "The coppers are coming for me!"

"You've got to stop watching those old gangster movies," laughed Rachel.

A fire truck zoomed by the house. Matthew breathed a sigh of relief. He slumped on the sofa.

"I think I need a mouthpiece," said Matthew. His parents looked confused. "You know…a lawyer. We need to have a family movie night, hopefully before they send me up the river. If I'm doing time in the big house, you'll have to learn the prison talk."

"Okay," said his father. "Let me get this straight. Nathan accidentally bumped into a police officer and you saw a man tear up a parking ticket. So, now the police are combing the streets looking for you."

"I think it's called a dragnet," explained Matthew.

"Can I rat on him?" asked Rachel.

Her parents looked at her.

"What?" said Rachel. "I'm a good sister. I'd visit him in the slammer."

"There's more," added Matthew. "Today at the park, I accidentally hit the officer with the Sizzle Saucer."

"I don't think anything you've done or seen would cause the police to be looking for you. Besides, you're such a good boy," said his mom as she squeezed his cheeks.

"Then why was the officer coming to arrest me during the saucer contest?" asked Matthew.

"He explained that to us when he gave Buster back," said his father. "He apologized. He saw Rail walk onto the field after digging some plates out of the trash can. He thought Rail was someone coming out of the stands to mess up your act."

"We told him your act was already a mess," said Rachel. "Rail was just bailing you out."

"By the way, the officer won third place for catching Buster," added his dad. "But, I'm not sure why Buster was all wet after the officer held him."

"Ok," argued Matthew, who wasn't at all convinced, "but why did that same officer come into the sporting goods store looking for me?"

"You said it was a sporting goods store customer that tore up the ticket. Maybe the officer was trying to find out who just bought a fishing pole. Sometimes stores have records, you know, checks or charge card receipts," his dad explained.

"So, I'm not on the lam?"

"No, but you may have gotten that officer's goat," laughed his dad.

Matthew suddenly felt relieved. He was a free man, or boy as the case may be. It was time to find Rail. Matthew couldn't wait to see the prizes they had won. He was now ready to collect his share. Matthew headed for the park. By the time he got there, most of the people had left.

Finally, he saw Stacy Lane. She was the prettiest girl in Matthew's class, at least he thought so. He would never admit it. Saying a girl is pretty when you're ten years-old can come with a heavy price – relentless teasing.

"Hi Matthew," said Stacy.

"Hi Stacy, have you seen Rail?"

"They went to the sporting goods store," answered Stacy.

"Hi Matthew," said Mrs. Lane, Stacy's mom. "We're going to the ice cream shop. Would you like to come along?"

"Yes, please come with us!" said Stacy.

Matthew looked into Stacy's eyes, "I'd love to." Suddenly he felt embarrassed, "Because I like ice cream."

"Great, I'll call your mom and tell her you're with us. We wouldn't want her to send the police out looking for you," said Mrs. Lane as she pulled a phone from her purse.

"No, I wouldn't want the police looking for me," Matthew laughed nervously.

Matthew walked downtown to the ice cream shop with Mrs. Lane and Stacy. It was near the sporting goods store. Matthew felt kind of special as he walked down the street with Stacy. She laughed at all of Matthew's jokes. It was nice getting all the attention from her.

That changed as they walked through the door of the ice cream shop. It seemed a lot of other people from the park had the same idea. Almost all the tables were full. Mr. Lane was waiting in a large booth. He waved his wife over. Matthew didn't expect Stacy's dad to be there. But, that wasn't the only surprise.

Mr. Lane was not alone. Matthew didn't see the other two people in the booth until he made his way through the crowd. Across from Mr. Lane sat Nathan and Rail. The chocolate mustache indicated that Nathan had started without them. Rail sipped a strawberry malt from a tall glass.

"Hi Matthew," said Mr. Lane. "I took the winners out for a little celebration."

"You mean winner, not winners," corrected Matthew. "Nathan didn't make it to the contest."

"Matthew left before the second half of our act," Nathan explained to Mr. Lane.

"You missed it," said Rail. "Nathan made it right after you left. Tossing Buster into the air to catch the saucer gave me an idea. I let Nathan toss me into the air to catch the saucer."

"We make a pretty good team, don't we little buddy," Nathan said to Rail. "Now we even have matching shoes."

"And matching flying discs," added Rail. "I've never had a real one before. I've always had to toss paper plates."

"You got new shoes?" Matthew asked Nathan.

Rail had Double Pump Slammers because Nathan had raised money from all his friends to pay for them. Now, Nathan won the shoes in the contest. Pretty soon, there would be nothing special about owning Double Pump Slammers, even the ones with sky blue soles.

"They're your shoes, too," Nathan said to Matthew. "Remember, the first big snowstorm, you can use them for skis."

Mr. Lane laughed.

Matthew shook his head, “I was only kidding about using your shoes for skis.”

“Well I have something just for you,” said Nathan. He pulled out the red Sizzle Saucer. “It’s all yours now. Rail and I won the new model, the Zippy Disc. It lights up when you throw it.”

Mrs. Lane looked at the line at the counter. “I wasn’t expecting this many people to be here. I’m afraid I’m running late for my meeting.” She looked at Mr. Lane. “Would you mind taking Matthew home after getting him some ice cream?”

“No problem,” said Mr. Lane.

“Good, the other boys should come with Stacy and me. Nathan’s mom is meeting me at the church to pick out the paint for the Sunday school rooms. Robert’s mom fixed a dress for Stacy. She needs to try it on.”

Mrs. Lane, Stacy, Nathan, and Rail stood to leave. Someone recognized the boys from the contest.

“It’s the big winners!” a voice called out. “We want a picture of your no-hands catch.”

Rail placed his new Zippy Disc in his mouth and posed. The room was filled with clicks and flashes as customers took pictures. Nathan and Rail took a bow.

Everyone cheered. People were giving them high fives. One little girl asked Rail to autograph a paper plate. Nathan and Rail were getting all the attention. Even Stacy seemed to be beaming as she walked with the two boys. It was the look she gave Matthew when she asked him to please have ice cream with her.

A path cleared out before them, which was really quite normal for Nathan. The pats on the back and handshakes were something new. Suddenly, Matthew was no longer in the mood for ice cream. Matthew had gone from the most wanted list to the not-even-noticed list in just a few hours.

Chapter 5

Turning Green

Matthew had determined something as he rode home with Mr. Lane. He stared at the red Sizzle Saucer. Matthew had decided he would not rest until he had mastered the art of disc tossing. He would be the greatest disc tosser in the whole world. It was his destiny!

He imagined himself standing on the podium. The national anthem was playing. He had just won the World Disc Tossing Olympics. He took the gold, silver, and bronze because no one was even close. Nathan and Rail watched, wishing they had even a fraction of the talent that Matthew used to dazzle the world.

"Matthew…Matthew," Mr. Lane's voice brought him back to reality. "This is your house, isn't it?"

Matthew suddenly realized the car had stopped.

"Uh…yes, thanks Mr. Lane," said Matthew.

He immediately headed for the backyard to start fulfilling his dream. He was on the path to destiny. Matthew began tossing the disc into the air and catching it.

"I'll show Nathan and Rail what a real disc tosser should look like. I'm going to be the best! They'll wish they had never tossed a Sizzle Saucer," he spoke out loud.

Matthew was concentrating so hard on the Sizzle Saucer that he didn't see the ladder.

"Look out," shouted Mr. Day.

The voice came from above Matthew. Mr. Day was painting some trim on the house. Matthew stopped right before hitting the ladder. The Sizzle Saucer zipped past the paint can. It came close to dumping green paint right on Matthew's head.

His father climbed down. "That was close. Another fraction of an inch and you would have been green with envy."

"N – V? New Vacuum?" asked Matthew.

"E-n-v-y, envy," said his dad.

"Oh," said Matthew, "I thought you were talking about how green you turned when you found out how much mom spent on the new vacuum."

"Don't remind me," said Mr. Day, "But that new vacuum did make your mom the envy of a lot of her friends." He chuckled, and then quickly became serious again. "Envy is wanting things that other people have, or in your case wanting to be better than them."

"What's wrong with that?" asked Matthew. "You always tell me to try to do my best."

"Sometimes it's not what you do, but why you do it," his father began to explain. "There's nothing wrong with wanting to be the best you can be. Sometimes that means being better than other people. King Solomon wrote in the book of Proverbs, "a heart of peace gives life to the body, but envy rots the bones."

"Being the best is something you should do to be an encouragement to others. You saw how people were entertained by Rail's paper plate throwing today. His skill made people happy. Envy crosses the line. It's when you feel so strongly about having something that you don't care about the people that you might hurt to get it. You trade things like love and friendship for possessions and false praise."

"False praise?" asked Matthew.

"It's those good things people say to you not because they mean it, but because it helps them in some way. You know, like when you tell me how great I am and then ask for a raise in your allowance."

"Well you are great, Dad," said Matthew, "but I try to limit the amount of times I tell you. I wouldn't want other people to envy you for having such an admiring son."

Matthew's dad rolled his eyes, "No, we wouldn't want that. But do you understand what I'm saying?"

"Sure," smiled Matthew. "If I envy people, I should drink lots of milk."

"What?" asked Mr. Day.

"Milk helps your bones get stronger. If envy causes your bones to rot, drink more milk," explained Matthew. "That King Solomon sure was wise."

Mr. Day sighed, "Tell me that's not all you got out of our talk."

Matthew smiled, "Ok, I was just teasing. Here it is in a nutshell. If I am only trying to be the best to make my friends feel bad, I'll only end up feeling worse about myself."

"Wow!" said Mr. Day, "You did get it! Now, tomorrow morning, go down to the park and practice throwing the disc because it's fun to develop some new skills. But don't loose one of the greatest skills you already have."

"What's that?" asked Matthew.

"Being a great friend," smiled Mr. Day.

Chapter 6

To Catch a Thief

Matthew and Buster practiced with the Sizzle Saucer in the park. The tosses were getting a little better. He felt a little less envious of Rail and Nathan after talking with his father the previous night. Still, he secretly hoped he could be better than them some day.

This time, he pictured himself on the podium. The national anthem played. Winning the gold medal in the World Disc Tossing Olympics was a wonderful feeling. Seeing his two best friends win the silver and bronze medals made it that much sweeter. Yes, there was enough glory to go around after all.

Suddenly, his daydreaming was interrupted by a woman screaming. "Help! Thief!"

Matthew looked around. A man emerged from a wooded area. He was running with a fishing pole. At the end of the pole was a woman's purse. It was such a strange sight that Matthew just stood and watched for a moment.

The man almost knocked Matthew over. There was something familiar about the man. Matthew recognized him from somewhere. The sporting goods store! It was the fisherman who tore up the parking ticket.

For some reason, Matthew started running after him. Nathan and Rail waved as Matthew ran by them. They were carrying their new Zippy Discs.

"Do you want to play?" yelled Nathan.

"Follow me!" pleaded Matthew. "Catch the thief!"

"Thief!" said Rail. "Let's go."

Now Matthew, Buster, Rail, and Nathan were chasing the man with the pole. The thief was running toward the river. The boys thought he probably had a get-away boat.

Buster caught up to the man. The pup wasn't that interested in the thief. He thought it would be great fun to grab the purse that was dangling on the pole. After one great leap, the thief had a big dog fish on the line.

The thief stopped and got into a tug-of-war with Buster. The pup thought that was lots of fun. The man suddenly saw the boys getting closer. He dropped the fishing pole and ran. Buster was disappointed that the fun had to end so soon. He sat by the purse and whimpered.

"He's getting away," said Rail. "We'll never catch him."

Suddenly Matthew had an idea. "Nathan, remember when you tripped me with the Sizzle Saucer in the park?"

"I'm on it," said Nathan.

The large boy stopped running. He took aim at the thief's legs. The Zippy Disc did the rest. The man tripped and rolled. He landed a foot from the edge of a cliff. The boys ran up to him.

The thief stood up. He had a very angry look on his face. Fear gripped the three boys. They never thought about what they would do when they caught the man. The thief clinched his fists and gritted his teeth.

Just as he was taking a step toward the boys, he suddenly disappeared. So did the ground beneath him. The edge of the cliff had broken off. The boys just looked at each other in disbelief.

"Is he dead?" asked Nathan.

"Help!" came a voice from somewhere over the cliff.

The policeman rushed up to the boys. "Stand back! The earth isn't stable. One false move and the whole side of that cliff could tumble into the river."

Soon rescue workers were on the scene. The boys almost felt bad they had chased the thief. He may not be a good person, but they wouldn't want him to be seriously hurt. They were also afraid the rescue workers might get hurt trying to save him. Matthew listened as the rescuers talked to each other.

"We can't risk climbing over the edge. It could start an avalanche. We tried tossing him a rope so he could be pulled up by a helicopter. He can't reach the rope and every time he moves, a little more of the cliff falls into the river," said one of the rescuers.

"Look at those clouds. If it starts to rain, it could start a mudslide. If only there was a way to get a rope to him," said another.

Matthew saw the fishing pole. Suddenly he had an idea. He picked up the pole. A sharp hook was at the end of the line. Matthew pushed the hook through the edge of his Sizzle Saucer.

"Use this," Matthew said to the rescuers. "You can throw the fishing line to him, and then tie on a heavier rope that he can pull over the ledge."

The rescue workers looked at each other.

"That just might work," one of the rescuers said as he looked at the Sizzle Saucer. "The only problem is I haven't thrown one of these in years. Are you any good at it?" he asked the other rescue worker.

The other worker frowned. "My friends tried to teach me, but I never quite mastered it."

They looked at Matthew.

"I'm not that good either, but I have two disc throwing champs with me," Matthew pointed at Nathan and Rail. "The big one throws hard, but the thin one is really good at trick throws."

"We need the trick throw," agreed the rescue workers as they took the saucer and walked over to Rail.

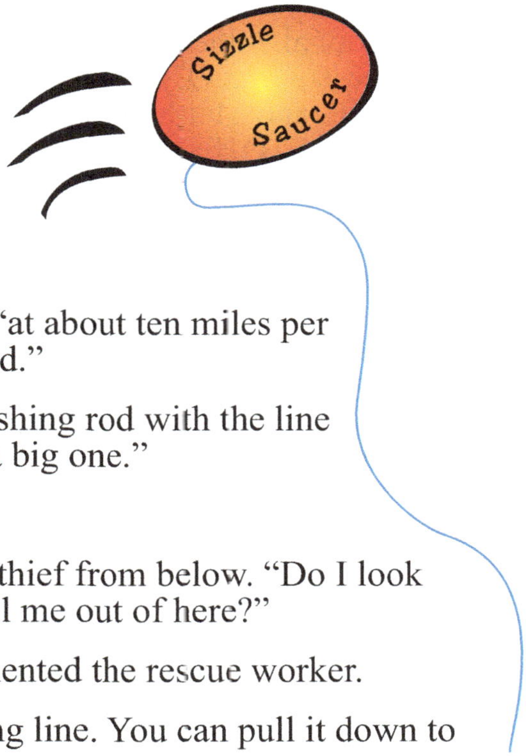

They took Rail near the cliff.

"How far down is he?" asked Rail.

"About 30 feet," said a rescuer.

Rail bent down and picked up some dried grass. He tossed it in the air.

"The wind is coming from the south," said Rail, "at about ten miles per hour. Make sure the fishing line is released on the rod."

"Check," said the rescuer who was holding the fishing rod with the line attached to the Sizzle Saucer. "Let's hope we catch a big one."

Rail made a perfectly calculated throw.

"A fishing line and a Sizzle Saucer," grunted the thief from below. "Do I look like a tuna fish? How about a rope big enough to pull me out of here?"

"He's not exactly the grateful type, is he?" commented the rescue worker.

"Hold on. We're tying a heavier rope to the fishing line. You can pull it down to you," a rescuer yelled to the thief.

Soon the helicopter lifted the thief off the cliff and deposited him on solid ground. The police were there to slap on the handcuffs. Matthew found out the "Fishing Pole Bandit" was wanted in several towns and even a few states. He used a fishing pole to snag purses.

"I guess he'll be going up the river to the big house," said Matthew to a rescue worker.

"Why do you think that man stole that lady's purse?" asked Rail.

Matthew smiled, "Envy."

"Envy?" asked Nathan.

"Yes," explained Matthew. "He probably envied people. Then, of course he had to steal money to buy milk. According to Solomon, envy is real hard on your bones."

"That makes sense to me," smiled Nathan.

"It does?" asked Matthew.

"Yes," said Nathan. "You have no idea why that man stole the purse, so you just made something up."

Matthew smiled. With his quick thinking, Nathan's hard throwing, and Rail's accurate tosses they made a pretty good flying disc team. He could just picture the three of them standing on a wide podium together.

The national anthem was playing. They had just won the World Disc Tossing Olympics – Team Event. Nathan, Rail, and Matthew were all proudly wearing their gold medals. His dad clapped wildly in the stands, happy that he had told his son all about the dangers of envy.

The boys walked past a police officer, the same one from the sporting goods store. The officer was standing near a "no parking" sign. He was writing a ticket for a car that was illegally parked. Matthew was caught in his Olympic daydream and bumped right into him. The officer dropped his ticket book.

"Boys," a rescue worker ran up to Matthew.

The rescuer was carrying the fishing pole and was going to give the Sizzle Saucer back to Matthew. Nathan turned around so suddenly that he knocked the rescuer off balance. The rescuer spun around with the fishing pole still in his hand. The bent-over police officer had just grabbed his ticket book. The fishing pole made a loud smacking sound right on the seat of the police officer's pants.

Poetry for the Senses

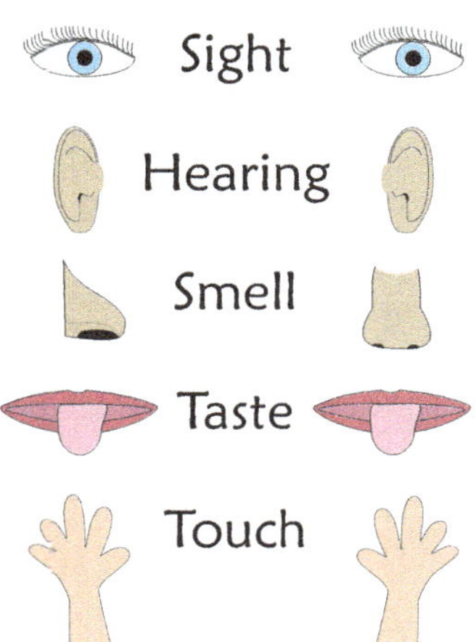

When you write, you can get the reader more involved in the story by describing things using as many senses as possible. This is also very important in poetry. We connect to the world using our five senses: sight, hearing, smell, taste, and touch. Sometimes you can use simple descriptions, or you might use a simile or metaphor.

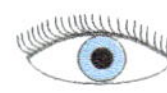 The puppy had big sad eyes and a shiny coat.

 The violin music sounded like a cat with its tail caught in a door.

 His stinky feet are rotten eggs.

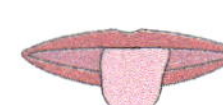 The hot cocoa was sweet with a touch of vanilla flavor.

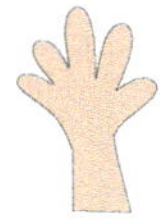 It felt like walking barefoot on a sidewalk on a hot summer day.

Read the poems below and the next page. Notice how senses are included and described.

Polecat

The black and white cat was warning me
A hiss alone should have made me flee
Its tail was soft and furry to the touch
But the odorous spray was way too much!

Striped Skunk by www.PDImages.com

Eating Oranges

My fingers dig into the peel
So cool and smooth to reveal
A taste so sweet on my tongue
With color like the golden sun

If a juicy squirt should hit my nose
It will delight like a fragrant rose
And if I should care to share a slice
A thankful voice will say I'm nice

Photo by Petr Kratochvil www.publicdomainpictures.net

Cookout

The smoky smell fills the air
Outdoor cooking adds a flair
My mouth waters in anticipation
For a delicious charcoal sensation

The sizzling sound from the grill
Dancing flames add to the thrill
A sip of ice cold sweet lemonade
Offsets the heat from the blaze

Any time it should be done
Ready to fill that soft fresh bun
Add on a cool crisp lettuce leaf
Slap pickles and ketchup on the beef

But the food is not the only treat
It's a family time that can't be beat
What I like best is all the smiles
That's all it takes to be worthwhile

The Case of the Malt-Eze Fountain

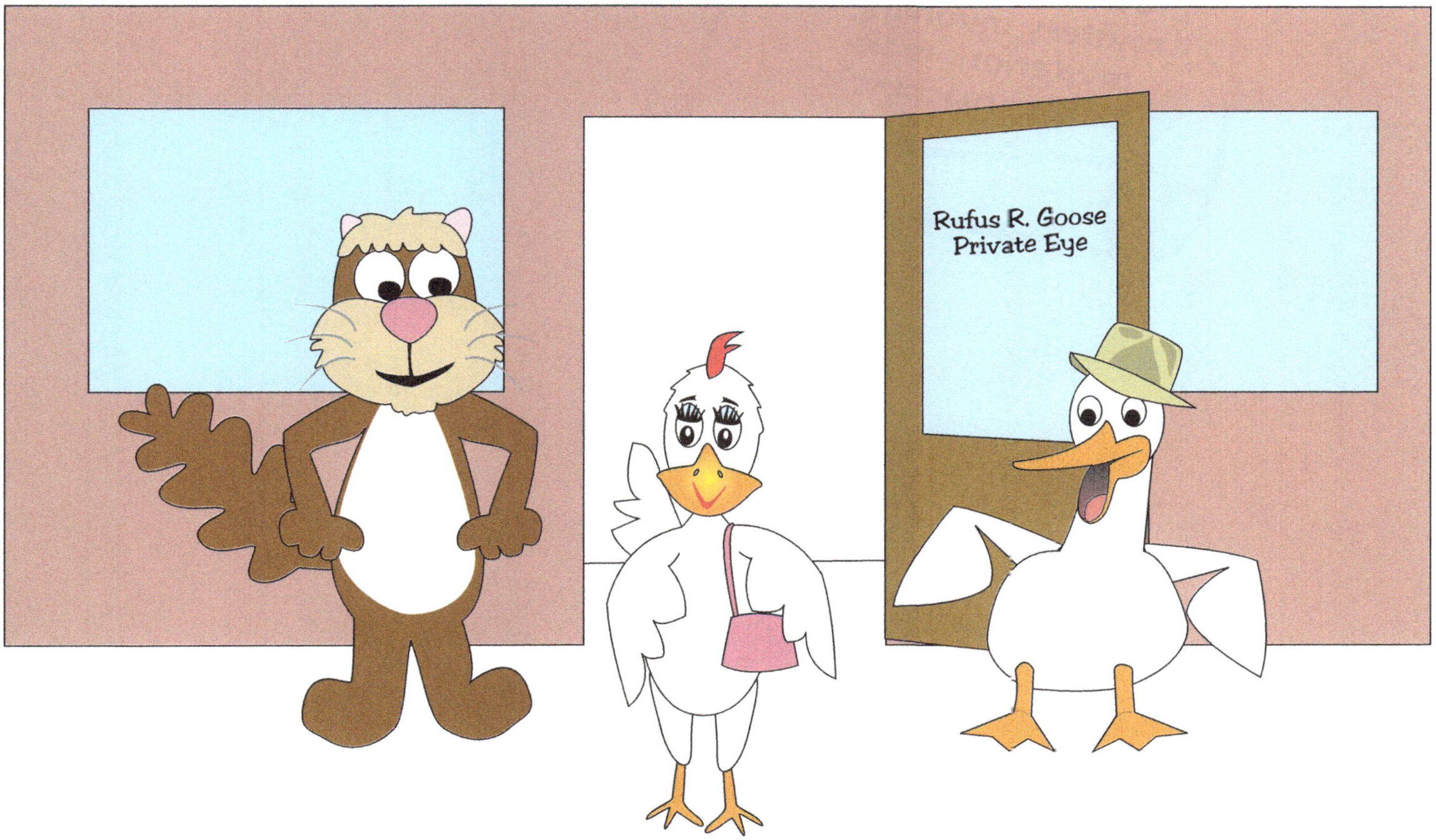

Story and illustrations by
Brian Davis

The Case of the Malt-Eze Fountain

When a beautiful, young chicken lures Puffy Paws the cat into tailing a rooster, things get ugly in a hurry. Will it leave Rufus R. Goose on his own as he solves a mystery involving a mysterious malt-making machine?

Vocabulary Words

delicious
destination
disguise
ferocious
impression
migrate
penthouse
rotund

Chapter 1

Ms. Wonderful

She was trouble the second she opened the door. If only Rufus R. Goose had known it was a sign of things to come, he may have not taken the case. The beautiful young hen known only as Ms. Wonderful opened the door. The door crashed into the ladder. Being on wheels, the ladder scooted across the room.

The startled goose ducked the ladder. It crashed into the wall. The box at the top of the ladder teetered on the edge. Rufus dived for the box. It was too late. "Pop, pop, pop!" crashed the box of light bulbs.

"They got me!" came a voice from near the ceiling as a big ball of fur plopped to the floor. "This is the last the world will see of poor old Puffy Paws."

"Oh my!" shouted the hen. "That poor cat landed on the floor!"

"Luckily I landed on my head," said the cat. "Unluckily I let go of the light after getting shot. I don't think I'm going to make it."

"You're not shot," said Rufus. "You heard the light bulbs breaking."

The cat looked himself over and smiled, "Good as new!" He popped to his feet.

"What a relief," sighed the hen. "But why is the ladder on wheels?"

"To change light bulbs," explained the cat.

"But why wheels?" asked Ms. Wonderful.

"It makes the ladder easier to move to screw in the light bulbs. One of us holds the light bulb. The other one turns the ladder. What else?" explained the cat.

"I guess that makes a whole lot more sense than turning the whole building," sighed Ms. Wonderful.

"Where were you the last time a bulb burned out?" asked Puffy Paws. "You could have saved us a lot of trial and error."

Rufus flapped his wings to lift above the broken glass. He landed on his desk. He motioned toward a chair and Ms. Wonderful sat down.

"How can we help you?" asked the goose.

"I must say, your ability to change a light bulb certainly makes an impression. I think you and your partner are just the kind of detectives I need to help me find my sister." explained the hen. "She flew the coop with a suave rooster named Boyd Thirsty. I'd like to find her and bring her back to the farm."

"We'll comb the city looking for the rooster," said Rufus. "Then we'll put a tail on him."

Puffy Paws purred, "I'm an expert on tails. See, mine's big and fluffy."

Ms. Wonderful patted Puffy Paws on the head. "You will do just fine. We won't need to comb the city. You can find him at the bird bath. I'll take Puffy and point out Thirsty."

"One more question for Puffy," said Ms. Wonderful. "Have you eaten today?"

Puffy frowned, "No."

"You must be starved. Maybe I can help you with some lunch." The beautiful chicken took Puffy by the paw and led him toward the door.

"What can I do?" asked Rufus.

"Clean the office and change the light bulb," suggested Ms. Wonderful.

"Who's going to turn the ladder?" asked Rufus.

"Why don't you buy self-twisting bulbs?" asked the chicken.

"That's a wonderful idea," said Rufus.

"What did you expect?" commented Ms. Wonderful.

Puffy picked up a box on his desk.

"What's with the box?" asked Ms. Wonderful as they walked down the street. "It doesn't have food in it does it?"

"No," answered Puffy. "It's my tail box. It contains all the equipment I need to tail a suspect."

"Does it include a gun?" asked Ms. Wonderful. "Boyd Thirsty could be dangerous. He has a sharp beak.

"It does, but I won't need it," explained Puffy Paws. "You see, I'm ferocious. I'm so ferocious " I sometimes scare myself."

"Oh yes," said Ms. Wonderful. "I noticed right away how ferocious you are. You're so big and handsome, too." The hen batted her eyes at the cat.

Puffy Paws grinned, "You're mighty pretty too, especially for a chicken."

"Thank you, Puffy Paws. You will protect me from that mean old Boyd Thirsty, won't you?"

"Yes, ma'am," answered Puffy Paws.

"But, I'm still so afraid. What if Boyd has friends? What if you're outnumbered? How would I be able to help you?" Ms. Wonderful patted the box Puffy was holding.

"I know," said Puffy Paws. "I've got just what you need in the box."

He opened the box. Ms. Wonderful smiled hopefully.
Puffy pulled something out. Suddenly the chicken looked disappointed.

"What is that?"

"It's my Puffy Paws mask. It looks just like me."

"What good is a disguise that looks just like you?" asked Ms. Wonderful.

Puffy put the mask on. "You think it might be me, but you don't know it's me, because it's a disguise. You can wear it and we'll be twice as ferocious."

Ms. Wonderful sighed. "I was thinking maybe I could hold the gun. That way if there's trouble I can fire it in the air and the police will come."

"Okay," said Puffy, "But my mask is pretty ferocious looking."

Ms. Wonderful tucked the gun into her purse. "Now I feel safe."

"I knew that once you thought about how ferocious the mask was, you would feel better. Would you like to wear it now?"

"I'll wait," said Ms. Wonderful. "I don't want to ruffle my feathers unless it's absolutely necessary. More importantly, we wouldn't want to terrorize the city."

"You're right," said Puffy. "I'll try to look harmless until we see Boyd."

"Yes, that's the look right there. Now you look very harmless," said Ms. Wonderful.

"No, this is still my ferocious face," corrected Puffy Paws.

Chapter 2

Tailing Thirsty

Puffy Paws and Ms. Wonderful arrived at the city bird bath. They sat on a park bench holding newspapers. They waited for hours. It was almost dark outside.

The chicken peaked over the top of the newspaper every few seconds. Puffy was totally distracted by his growling stomach.

“I’m awfully hungry. Why don’t I go get us a little snack?” suggested Puffy.

“No need,” said Ms. Wonderful. “There he is, over there.”

“The hot dog stand? That’s a great idea,” said Puffy.

“Not hot dogs. Look at the rooster over there. It’s Thirsty, that big delicious looking bird. He’s heading for that dark alley. Go eat him. I mean tail him.”

Puffy Paws grabbed his box and ran after the rooster. Ms. Wonderful smiled and followed from a distance. Her wing was tucked in her purse as she reached the dark alley. In the darkness she heard a loud squawking, then hissing and shrieking.

Bang! Bang! Bang! Bang! The shots rang out. Then, everything fell silent in the alley.

“Puffy Paws? Boyd? Are you alright?”

There was nothing but silence. The only sound was the sound of the gun sliding on the ground.

Ms. Wonderful ran down the street calling out for help. A police duck flapped down the street. The chicken pointed to the alley.

“It’s terrible,” she cried. “They’re both dead.”

A flock gathered at the alley. The police ducks pushed the crowd back. An ambulance crew pushed its way through.

"It's a mess in there," a police duck told the ambulance crew. "Be careful. It's a very sticky situation."

"Where's that chicken?" asked another police duck. "Maybe she can tell us what happened."

Ms. Wonderful slipped through the crowd and disappeared from sight unnoticed.

Meanwhile, back at the office, Rufus R. Goose was busy on the phone. He had been calling light bulb shops all day, asking about self-twisting light bulbs. No one had even heard of them.

He was so distracted on the phone; Rufus didn't notice the shadowy figure outside his door. Someone was very interested in the phone calls Rufus was making.

"Special delivery!" cried the voice outside the door.

A letter slipped through the mail slot in the door. It dropped to the floor. Rufus waddled over and picked it up. He slipped open the envelope and smiled. The goose slipped on his hat and jacket then quickly left the office.

Rufus gave the cab driver directions. The raccoon cab driver was confused when he arrived at the destination. So was the goose as he stared at the vacant lot.

"The ad said this was the place," said the Goose. "See," Rufus handed the raccoon the ad that had been dropped off at his office.

The raccoon studied the ad, "Self-twisting light bulb sale? This is the address on the sale ad. I think you've been led on a wild goose chase."

"Oh, those wild geese!" honked Rufus. "They're so frustrating. They budge into the food line at all our family reunions."

On the cab ride back to the office, Rufus pondered which relative could have sent him on the wild goose chase. If he found out, they would be sorry. He would make sure their invitation to the next family reunion got lost. Maybe all the invitations to wild geese should get lost.

He was still mumbling to himself as he trudged up the steps. Rufus didn't notice the two police duck-tectives waiting at his office door. He almost bumped into them as they blocked the doorway.

"We need to talk to you Goose," said a police duck-tective.

"I need to talk to you," said Rufus. "Someone sent me false advertising!"

"That's serious," said the other duck-tective. "When did this happen?"

"Marvy!" said the other duck-tective "We're here about a murder!"

"I guess that is more serious, Harvey" said Marvy, "Almost as bad as trying to buy self-twisting light bulbs without a permit."

Rufus gulped and quickly changed the subject, "You wanted to talk to me about a murder?"

"Oh yes," said Harvey. "A cat has been murdered."

"Eaten by a rooster," added Marvy. "There's not much left." He held out a cardboard box.

Rufus looked in the box. All he saw was a face and a tail. It looked too familiar.

"Puffy?" whimpered Rufus as he stumbled to the floor in agony.

"It's not a pretty sight, I know," said Harvey.

"Then again, Puffy never was a pretty sight," added Marvey.

Harvey held out a gun. "Is this yours?"

"Yes," said Rufus.

"I see," said Harvey. "Where were you at 6:00 tonight?"

"Me?" questioned Rufus. "You think I had something to do with this? Are you a couple of loons?"

"No," answered Marvey. "But a loon is an aquatic bird that looks a lot like a duck, so we understand the confusion."

"Still," said Harvey, "You would think a goose would know the difference."

"I meant are you crazy?" corrected Rufus.

"That's between me and my therapist," said Marvey.

"We're still being evaluated," added Harvey.

Rufus sighed, "I would never hurt Puffy. What about the rooster?"

"Thirsty's not talking," said Harvey.

"Boyd Thirsty?" asked Rufus.

"Do you know him?" asked Marvey.

"No," said Rufus. "Puffy was tailing him for a client. Before he was…"

The goose started honking sadly. The duck-tectives patted him on the back. They started quacking sadly. After a good cry, the ducks were ready to leave.

"You don't need to come to the station tonight," said Harvey.

"But don't migrate until our investigation is over," added Marvey.

"I'm not going anywhere until I get justice for Puffy," Rufus vowed.

The duck-tectives left. Rufus walked into his dark office. He didn't even bother to turn on his light. It wouldn't have mattered anyway. It was burned out. The goose slumped into his office chair and closed his eyes.

Suddenly, he felt a cold metal object pressed to his head. The goose slowly sat up in his chair.

"Good evening, Mr. Goose," said a strange voice.

Chapter 3

A Light in the Darkness

"Who are you?" asked Rufus.

"Sparrow, Joe Sparrow," answered the small bird as he pressed the gun to the goose's head. "I'm here to search your office. I've been waiting for the two duck-tectives to leave. They came right after I sent you on that wild goose chase."

"That was you!" exclaimed Rufus. "Don't tell anyone."

"I understand. It would be embarrassing for a super private eye to be tricked so easily," said Sparrow.

"No," said Rufus. "I want to keep blaming my wild relatives so they don't get invited to the family reunion."

Sparrow pushed the gun harder to the goose's head. "Enough chirp chat. I need to search your office."

"Go ahead," said Rufus. "You do know that isn't a real gun. It's a flashlight and it's not too bright. If you want to search my office, you'll need to change the light bulb. Can you trust me to turn the ladder for you?"

"Turn the ladder?" questioned Joe Sparrow. "Why not just twist the light bulb to screw it into the socket?"

"Twist the light bulb!" laughed Rufus. "What a silly idea. Are you going to send me on a wild goose chase to get manual twisting light bulbs?"

"I bought some manual twisting light bulbs at the store down in the lobby of this building," said Joe, "right after you left. They were on the shelf next to the self-twisting light bulbs."

"Then why didn't you buy those?" asked Rufus.

"I didn't have a permit," explained Joe.

"Oh," sighed Rufus. "Still how are you going to…"

Click! Suddenly the room was bright. Joe Sparrow fluttered down from the light fixture. He landed on Rufus' shoulder.

"Now, I'm going to search your office."

"Go ahead," said Rufus. "But, I'm warning you, it's a mess. If you just tell me what you're looking for, maybe I can steer you right to it."

"You mean Birdie didn't leave it here?" said Joe.

"I don't even know who Birdie is," said Rufus.

"Birdie O'Henesee, the good-looking chicken that was here this morning. I followed her here. Did she leave a package with you?"

"You mean she isn't Ms. Wonderful?"

Sparrow laughed, "There's nothing wonderful about that bird. I'd be careful with her. She was the last one to see your puffy partner alive."

The sparrow noticed the sorrowful look on the face of the goose. "I think you're telling the truth. Maybe the chicken doesn't have the package. If you can help me find it, there's $5,000 in it for you, and maybe you can get to the bottom of the cat's demise."

Rufus didn't care about the money. He did care about justice. The goose wanted to solve this case and put Puffy's murderer away for good.

"What should I do?" asked Rufus.

"Set up a meeting with Birdie and me," said Sparrow.

"I will under one condition," said Rufus.

"What's that?" said Sparrow.

"Show me how you replaced that light bulb!" honked Rufus.

The next morning, Rufus went to the hotel room of Ms. Wonderful, who he now knew was really Birdie O'Henesee. He was angry and confused. He thought the chicken was so beautiful. He wanted to believe she was good. He even wanted to believe she liked him. She had a certain "gooseness" about her that he found attractive.

If only she were innocent, maybe they could have a future together. Maybe her love could fill the emptiness he felt over losing his friend Puffy Paws. He had to keep his head clear. Still his heart was very heavy.

"I don't feel you've been honest with me," Rufus confronted Birdie.

The nervous chicken tried to act innocent, "Whatever do you mean?"

"I didn't need self-twisting light bulbs. All I needed to do was to screw in manual twisting light bulbs."

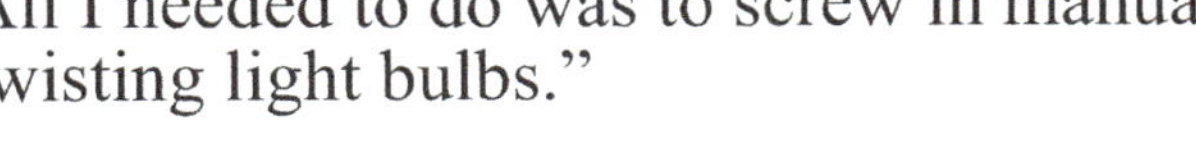

“Oh that,” sighed Birdie. “I thought you discovered I really wasn’t Ms. Wonderful. Oops…”

“That too,” said Rufus. “I know your name is really Birdie O’Henesee.”

The chicken gasped, “How did you ever find out?”

“A little birdie told me, a sparrow,” Rufus watched for a reaction.

He saw the look of surprise on the hen’s face. He was on to something.

“I don’t know anyone named Joe Sparrow,” denied Birdie.

“Then how did you know his name was Joe?” asked Rufus.

“Uh…a wild guess?” Birdie tried to explain.

“A wild guess? Wolfgang Sparrow is a wild guess. Tiger Sparrow is a wild guess. Joe Sparrow is a rather tame guess.”

“Oh, I just can’t lie to you,” said Birdie. “I came to you because I’m a big fan of yours. I’ve secretly loved you from afar. I told you my name was Ms. Wonderful, just because I wanted to hear those words from your beak. I wanted to be your Ms. Wonderful!”

“Maybe you are in love with me. I am rather irresistible. Still, you’ve not been honest with me. I can’t be too sure you are telling the truth until I know whoever is responsible for Puffy Paws gets justice.”

“I’m not sure I have the answers you need,” said Birdie, “but if I could talk to Joe Sparrow, maybe I could help you.”

“He’s already told me how to screw in a light bulb,” answered Rufus.

“I mean with Puffy Paws,” said Birdie.

“Oh, that would be helpful. I’ll call him and have him meet us at my apartment.”

As Rufus and Birdie neared his apartment his acute observational skills kicked in. He suspected they were being watched. They ducked into his apartment. The quacking seemed to momentarily confuse the suspected spy.

They flapped to the second floor apartment. Rufus quickly opened the door. He stared out the window. The goose called Birdie over.

“I think we’re being watched,” said Rufus. “Do you recognize him?”

“Which one?” asked Birdie.

“The one looking through binoculars staring up at us,” answered Rufus.

“I got an idea,” said Birdie.

She took a piece of paper and scribbled something on it. She held it up to the window. Rufus saw the watcher shake his head no. Birdie handed the paper to Rufus. He read it: Are You Spying On Us?

"I guess he's not spying on us," said Rufus. "He did shake his head no."

"Technically, we were spying on him then," noted Birdie.

"If we only knew why we were spying on him, maybe we could get some answers. I'll go talk to him."

Rufus opened the door. He almost stepped on Joe Sparrow. The mysterious bird they were spying on would have to wait. Rufus went back inside.

Chapter 4

Two Meetings

Joe and Birdie looked at each other.

"I don't have it," said Joe. "Do you have it?"

"I don't have it," answered Birdie. "I thought you had it."

Rufus was beginning to suspect that Joe and Birdie had met before.

"Who do you *think* has it?" asked Joe.

"Who do *you* think has it?" asked Birdie.

"I think Duckman has it," answered Joe.

"I think you're right. Duckman must have it," said Birdie.

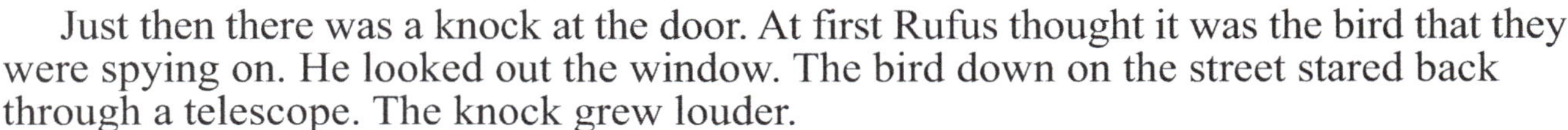

Just then there was a knock at the door. At first Rufus thought it was the bird that they were spying on. He looked out the window. The bird down on the street stared back through a telescope. The knock grew louder.

He motioned for Joe and Birdie to get quiet. Joe carefully closed the door to the room behind him before opening the door to the hallway. It was best that no one know about his mysterious guests.

Rufus opened the door. In the hallway stood the two duck-tectives, Marvey and Harvey. They were trying to peek over his shoulder into his apartment. Rufus spread his wings to block their view.

"Can we come in?" asked Harvey.

"Sure, if you have a search warrant," answered Rufus.

"I have a feeling you know something you're not telling us," said Marvey.

"There is something," admitted Rufus. "You can screw in light bulbs."

"I knew it!" said Harvey. "You'll have to come to the station with us."

"For more questioning?" asked Rufus.

"No," said Harvey, "To change light bulbs. We have a bunch that are burnt out and our ladder has a locked-up wheel."

"I accidentally shut it in one of the cells," admitted Marvey.

Just then there was a loud chirping from behind Rufus. That was followed by loud squawking. The two duck-tectives charged past Rufus. They entered the room behind him.

"What's going on in here?" demanded the ducks.

"She pecked me," said Joe Sparrow as he rubbed his head.

"He whistled at my drumsticks," accused Birdie.

"I think we need to take you three birds down to the station to straighten all this out."

"What a minute," said Rufus. "I think you're confused about what is happening here. We're rehearsing a play."

Harvey crossed his wings. He doubted the goose. "Well?" he stared at the other two birds.

"That's right," sighed Joe, "Pretty realistic pecking." He continued rubbing his head.

"Pretty realistic drumsticks," said Birdie. She pointed to her leg and batted her eyes at the duck-tectives.

Rufus stepped in. "It's all an act. Nevertheless, you might want to take Mr. Sparrow down to the station. He's the one who taught me how to change a light bulb."

The duck-tectives eyes brightened. They each grabbed a sparrow wing and carried Joe out the door.

"You ungrateful goose!" shouted Joe from the hallway.

"We'll talk in the morning," Rufus honked back.

Birdie took a cab back to her hotel. Rufus grabbed a piece of paper. He scribbled a message on it. The goose held it up to his window. The spy on the street read the note through the telescope; I'm Going To Bed Now. I'll Spy on You Again Tomorrow. The spy took his telescope and walked into the hotel across the street.

The next morning, Rufus entered the hotel. He was relieved to see he wasn't too early. He suspected the bird behind the newspaper was the same one who he was watching the day before. The newspaper was suspicious. It was just a feeling a great private eye like Rufus had.

Maybe it was the large hole with a telephoto lens sticking out that the Goose picked up on. It could have been the tripod legs sticking out from the beneath paper. Perhaps the fact that the paper was held upside down drew his attention. It may have even been the clicking sound and the bright flash that caught his attention. Whatever it was, Rufus almost had the feeling he was being photographed.

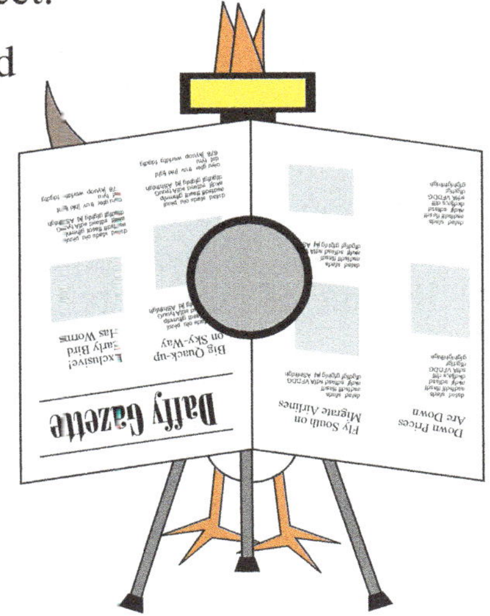

Rufus pulled the paper down. Behind it was a cuckoo with a camera. The bird smiled meekly at the goose and snapped another picture.

"Who are you and why have I been spying on you?" demanded Rufus.

"Wilber Cuckoo," answered the photographer. "You want me to take you to Quacker Duckman."

"Yes!" honked Rufus, "That must be it. I'd also like double prints of those photos if they turn out well. Do you have two hour developing?"

"If all goes well with Duckman, I think something can be arranged," said Wilber. "Follow me."

The two birds took the elevator to the top floor. The birds walked to the door of the penthouse apartment. It was very large and fancy. It was a good thing the room was large, because Quacker Duckman was a rather chubby duck.

"My dear Rufus," Duckman talked to him like he was a long lost friend. "I'm so glad you accepted my invitation. Would you like some gooseberry juice?"

Rufus nodded yes and took the glass from the rotund duck. He sat on a couch. Duckman sat in a heavily reinforced chair.

"I suppose you're wondering why I asked you here," said Quacker Duckman. Rufus nodded. "You've been spending time with some birds that have a mutual interest. It is an interest that may have led to the untimely demise of you're furry friend."

The duck had the goose's full attention. Rufus thought he may have been finally getting somewhere.

"We're all looking for the same package, Birdie, Joe Sparrow, and me. How much are they paying you?" asked Quacker.

"That's between me and my clients," said Rufus.

"I'll pay you $25,000 if you find it for me. Plus you can get added benefits."

"Added benefits?" asked Rufus. "What do you mean?"

"You don't know what's in the package?" smiled Duckman. His belly jiggled as he laughed. "It's very valuable. Even I don't know how much it could be worth. What's a lifetime of chocolate salmon malts worth?"

"I don't care. I just want information about Puffy Paws," answered Rufus.

"In due time," said Duckman. "But, you must get the package first."

"Okay," Rufus decided to play along. "What's in the package?"

Quacker took a sip of gooseberry juice and leaned forward to tell his story.

Chapter 5

Quacker Duckman

"I've searched for the contents of the package for the last fifteen years. If I can just get my wings on it, it will have been worth the wait. It would have been worth all the sacrifice," Quacker Duckman began his tale.

Rufus honked angrily, "Not worth the sacrifice of Puffy Paws!"

"Calm down, you silly goose. I didn't mean your friend. I meant my sacrifice. My time and the money I paid to hire those traitors!"

"What traitors?" Rufus calmed down.

"Birdie O'Henesee, Joe Sparrow, even Boyd Thirsty" answered Quacker. "They all want my prize."

"And what is this mystery prize?" asked Rufus.

"It all started two hundred years ago. There was a kingfisher in Spain that grew tired of hovering over the water looking for fish. It was all very tedious. What he really loved was a good salmon flavored malt.

A little milk, ice cream, malt powder, chocolate syrup, and a fresh salmon, who could resist? It was his dream to open up his own fly-in restaurant and serve his special, delightful drink. He spent years perfecting his drink and the machine to make it.

Finally, it was finished. The kingfisher opened his restaurant. It was a great success. The machine worked perfect. Not only did it make great malts, it was also easy to use. You just add all the ingredients and the machine does all the rest. It is that machine I have relentlessly pursued. It is called the Malt-Eze Fountain. I need it before I waste away to feather and bones."

"I think we have some time," said Rufus. "But what happened to the Malt-Eze Fountain?"

"The kingfisher eventually died. Through the years his children and grandchildren took over the fly-in restaurant. One day, the fountain just disappeared. It is believed that one of the kingfishers sold it to pay his creditors. Have you ever seen a kingfisher? The all have big bills."

Rufus honked, "Don't we all?"

"The machine was lost for over a hundred years. It was painted over with black paint. A collector thought it was some falcon statue. Can you believe that? By the time I tracked it down, it had been sold to a private individual in Russia.

When that individual would not sell it to me, I had my employees appropriate it."

"You mean steal it!" honked Rufus.

"That was not as big a crime as putting that precious fountain in a glass case simply to be looked at. Have you ever tasted a perfectly made chocolate salmon malt? It's like a scoop of heaven in your beak. If the world gets a taste of it, I'll be rich. The machine really hasn't rightfully belonged to anyone since in was stolen a hundred years ago.

I'll share those riches with you only if you will help me get the Malt-Eze Fountain."

"So, my friend was killed so you could have salmon malts? Is that what Puffy's life was worth? I'm sorry Duckman. I can't be a part of this!"

Rufus Goose stormed out of the hotel. He went to his office. The goose honked sadly. He missed Puffy Paws. He started crying.

"Poor Puffy Paws, eaten by a rooster. Boo hoo, hoo! He was so full of life," cried Rufus.

"Boo, hoo, hoo! And so ferocious, and handsome," added a sniffling voice from another part of the room. "I'm really going to miss me. My life won't be the same without me. Boo, hoo, hoo!"

Rufus stopped crying. "Puffy Paws? Is that you?"

The chair from the other desk spun around. A big furry cat was holding a newspaper.

"Did you read the front page? I'm dead. Why didn't anyone tell me? Did I miss my funeral?"

Rufus' beak dropped to the floor. "You're alive!"

"But it's in the newspaper," protested Puffy Paws.

"How can this be?" asked Rufus.

"I guess some reporter found out I was dead," said Puffy Paws.

The goose checked the cat's pulse. "You're not dead, Puffy! Where have you been?"

"I've been in jail," said Puffy Paws.

"Why?" asked Rufus.

"Because that's where Boyd Thirsty is."

Rufus sighed. "Tell me the whole story."

“Well,” explained Puffy. “I followed Boyd Thirsty into the dark alley. When I tried to tail him, he got upset. He wouldn’t let me tie the tail on him. It was dark in the ally, so he probably couldn’t tell it was the nice, fluffy one just like mine.

He started squawking. I started hissing. The next thing I know, I hear the bang, bang, bang, bang of a gun. I jumped into a dumpster. I’m not sure what happened in the alley. You see the dumpster had some really good scraps, and I was very hungry.

I hadn’t eaten all day. Ms. Wonderful kept telling me how delicious rooster tasted. But, I kept thinking that rooster must taste like chicken, and you know I’m not a big chicken fan. There was fresh salmon in the dumpster that was just so tasty. It couldn’t have been in there for more than a week. After a good meal, there’s nothing like a good catnap. When I woke from my nap, I found my tail box.”

Puffy lifted the box onto his desk. “My Puffy Paws mask was missing and that made me really sad. One of my fake tails was missing too.”

“That’s what was in the duck-tectives bags,” said Rufus. It was all coming together.

“I turned on the tracker beacon for the tail I tied to the rooster. It led right to the police station. I went inside, but the ducks wouldn’t let me back into the jail cells to keep an eye on Boyd Thirsty.

So I had a plan. I went out and tried to buy a self-twisting light bulb without first getting a permit. So, I was arrested and put into the jail cell right across from Boyd Thirsty. Sadly, I had to get out of jail today. The penalty for trying to buy a self-twisting light bulb without a permit is only spending 24 hours in jail.”

“Did Boyd Thirsty say anything to you?” asked Rufus.

“Of course not,” said Puffy. “It may have been the gumball stuck in his throat, or maybe it was because I was dead.”

“I would stick with the gumball theory,” said Rufus.

The goose dug through the tail box. “Where is the gumball gun?”

“I gave it to Ms. Wonderful. She wanted to feel safe. If there was trouble she was going to fire it into the air,” explained Puffy.

“Or, into a rooster and a cat,” sighed Rufus.

Chapter 6

A Special Delivery

Rufus was trying to figure everything out when he heard a desperate squawk outside the door. He opened it to find a large bird in a ship captain's cap. It had a package in its beak. The pelican coughed and the package slid onto the floor.

The bird struggled through the door. It plopped down on a sofa in the office waiting area. That's when Rufus noticed the red ooze below the bird's wing. It sighed heavily and closed its eyes. The large bird was completely still.

"I think he's dead," said Rufus.

"Been there, done that," commented Puffy Paws.

Rufus reached for the bird's wallet. He opened it up. The goose unfolded a piece of paper and studied it.

"It says his name is Jacob B. Shearwater. He's the captain of a ship called the S. S. Puffinus."

Rufus tossed the paper on a table and backed up. He almost fell over something. It was a package wrapped in paper and tape. The goose had a good idea what it was.

"Get a box from the storeroom."

The goose packed the wrapped object into the box. He taped it up and wrote an address on it.

"Puffy, I need you to stay out of sight a little longer. Stay here and don't answer the door. The world needs to think you're dead for just a little while longer."

"Poor world," sighed Puffy Paws.

Rufus took the box to the United Pelican Store next to his office. He scheduled the package to be delivered the next morning. Next, he went back to see Quacker Duckman. Wilber Cuckoo saw him at the elevator and tried to stop him.

The goose bowled the cuckoo over and stormed into Duckman's room.

"Meet me at my apartment at 9:30 tomorrow morning." The goose quacked in his most angry tone. "I'll have your precious malt-eze fountain! Make sure you have my money. Bring Joe Sparrow and Wilber Cuckoo with you."

Rufus smiled when he reached the elevator. The trap was set. Next, he went to see Birdie O'Henesee. She hugged him when she opened the door.

"My dear goose, do you have good news for me?"

"I'll have the package at my apartment tomorrow morning. Be there by 9:30," said Rufus.

The next day, Quacker Duckman, Joe Sparrow, Wilber Cuckoo, and Birdie O'Henesee met at the apartment of Rufus R. Goose promptly at 9:30 am.

"Where's the machine?" asked Duckman.

"First things first," said Rufus. "There's a matter of murder: Boyd Thirsty, Puffy Paws, and Captain Jacob B. Shearwater. I don't want the police blaming me. We need someone here to take the blame, maybe the one who did it?"

"Wilber shot the captain. Puffy Paws and Thirsty I know nothing about," said Quacker.

"Then the police might just blame you," explained Rufus.

"How about the cuckoo? He's crazy," offered Joe Sparrow.

"That's a good idea," agreed Birdie.

"Yeah, let's blame the cuckoo," agreed Wilber. "Wait a minute, I'm the cuckoo."

"Good, we all agree," said Rufus. "Now, I believe there is a matter of $25,000 that is owed me."

Quacker pulled out an envelope. Inside was $10,000. "This will have to do," said the rotund duck.

"It's a little short," argued Rufus. "Where's the rest?"

"In due time," assured Quacker. "I need *some* money to start the fly-in restaurant. Soon we'll have all the cash we need."

The door bell rang exactly at 10:00. A pelican wearing brown shorts stood at the door holding a box. The birds quickly cleared off a table. They quickly tore open the box.

Wilber looked through the packing material. “There’s no packing slip!”

The other birds sighed. Rufus handed Quacker a pair of scissors. He quickly, but carefully cut through the tape and paper wrap around the fountain.

The duck set it on the table and studied it. “I’ve got to see if it is the real thing.”

He scratched off some black paint. The birds flocked around the machine. C-o-f-f-E-z-e. The duck stopped and looked up.

He smiled a little, “It’s not the Malt-Eze Fountain. This is the Coff-Eze Cappuccino Machine. I have no use for it.”

The duck turned to Rufus, “I’m afraid I’m going to have to ask for my money back.”

“I brought you the package, just as you asked. It’s not my fault you stole the wrong machine.”

“That’s true, but we all have to share in the loss. I’m going to need that money to keep looking for the elusive malt machine.”

Rufus handed almost all the money over. He kept back $10. “It’s for expenses,” the goose explained.

“Fair enough,” smiled Quacker. “Our next stop on the quest is Turkey.”

“The country?” asked Joe Sparrow.

“No, the turkey farm on the edge of town. There’s an old Tom turkey that might know of the next place for us to look.”

He tipped his hat to Rufus, “It’s been a pleasure doing business with you. Now we must go back to the hotel and pack.”

Joe Sparrow and Wilber Cuckoo followed him out the door.

Chapter 7

Coff-eze Anyone?

"We're still going to blame everything on Wilber, right?" Birdie asked Rufus when they were alone. "This will be so wonderful. We can migrate south for the winter together. We can set up a little coffee shop and make all kinds of money from the Coff-eze Cappuccino Machine. It will be perfect."

"Yes, dear, but chickens don't migrate," frowned Rufus.

He picked up the phone. "I need to speak to Duck-tectives Harvey and Marvey. There's a whole bunch of thieves and crooks in the penthouse of the Falcon Crest Hotel across from my apartment. There's one more here. She tried to kill Puffy Paws and Boyd Thirsty."

Rufus hung up the phone.

Birdie looked terrified, "You're not turning me in. How could you?"

"Let me explain it. You tried to kill Boyd Thirsty and blame the murder on Puffy Paws. Don't deny it. You had his gun. You knew Thirsty wouldn't be at the birdbath until evening. You picked up Puffy Paws in the morning, knowing he would get hungrier and hungrier during the day. You tried filling the cat's head with thoughts of eating a certain rooster. What you didn't know is that Puffy's head holds very little. The smell of week-old salmon drove any thoughts of a rooster sandwich right out of that cat's mind.

You tried to think of everything. Your backup plan was to take care of the rooster yourself. You shot him with Puffy's gun. What you didn't know is that it was a gumball gun. We matched the gumballs found in the ally to the gun. When Puffy didn't eat the rooster, you shot Thirsty twice and tried to shoot Puffy too.

You wanted it to look like Puffy shot Thirsty and then accidentally shot himself. You just couldn't see in the dark alley that Puffy was already dumpster diving."

We would have known it was you sooner, but a gumball landed in Thirsty's throat. It took a few days, but the gum finally softened. Once Thirsty blew a bubble, he was ready to talk. You set him up. You told him to meet you in that alley."

"How can you say that? Don't even pretend," clucked Birdie.

“Maybe I love you, and maybe you love you too, but I could never trust you,” said Rufus coldly.

“I do love me, I truly do!” pleaded Birdie.

“I can never forget you tried to kill Puffy Paws,” said Rufus.

“Is it because I didn’t succeed? Do you hate me so because I am a failure?” cried Birdie.

“I couldn’t love you now if you were a success *and* a goose,” said Rufus. “It’s too late for us.”

It was indeed too late. Duck-tectives Harvey and Marvey stormed through the door with several police ducks.

“We got the others,” said Harvey.

The police wing-cuffed Birdie and led her away. Rufus gave Harvey the money he took from Quacker Duckman.

Marvey picked up the fountain, “What’s this?”

“The stuff that drinks are made from,” sighed Rufus.

When Rufus got back to the office he smelled hot food as he reached for the doorknob. Inside the office Puffy was just taking a tray of French fries out of the toaster oven. What the goose saw next really shocked him. Captain Jacob B. Shearwater had pulled a chair up next to Puffy.

“It turns out the captain wasn’t dead after all,” explained Puffy. “He had fallen on a ketchup bottle in the hallway. I left it there by accident last week. The fall only knocked him out. What’s ketchup without fries?” asked Puffy as he dipped a fry in the red blotch on the captain’s chest.

The goose placed the Coff-eze Cappuccino Machine on his desk.

“Do we get to keep it?” asked Puffy.

“No,” explained Rufus. “I sold it to a starling and two ducks. It’s the only money we’re making off this case. They want to use it to start a new a coffee shop.”

Puffy poured some coffee from the machine. “This makes great coffee,” said the cat. “I’m sure they’ll make lots of money.”

“I doubt it,” said Rufus. “Not with a goofy name like Starducks.”

Super Pork and the Three Little Pigs

Story and illustrations by
Brian Davis

The Malt-Eze Fountain was a *parody* of an old movie and book called *The Maltese Falcon*. It was a story about a private eye named Sam Spade. A *parody* is a kind of story that imitates another story or a type of story in a humorous way. *Super Pork and the Three Little Pigs* is another parody. It imitates the story of the *Three Little Pigs* as well as super heroes in general.

As you read this story, think of how it is like the *Three Little Pigs* and how it is different from the *Three Little Pigs* story that you're used to. Also, compare Super Pork to other super heroes.

Vocabulary Words

application
bewildered
communication
compartment
dispatcher
grant
interrupted
monitoring
perfection
specific

Chapter 1

Super Problem

Mort the pig wallowed happily in the mud. It was just the way he liked it, not too watery and not too thick. The cool ooze was just what was needed on a hot summer day. To him, his little pen was pig paradise.

Life on the farm was a perfect as it could get. The problem with perfection is that the least little thing can make everything imperfect. That's what Mort was soon to find out. Only, the problem he would soon face was not a small one.

Mort's playful romp was soon interrupted by a ringing bell. The pig immediately scurried to the hogwash. It was his own private shower he used to clean off the mud. It washed the mud back into his pen right where it belonged.

A flock of blue birds swarmed over the pig. They had heard the bell, too. They knew exactly what to do. The birds carried a red shirt and cape. Mort quickly changed.

"Super Pork to the rescue!" shouted Mort.

The birds chirped excitedly. Each bird began tugging at Super Pork. Soon, the pig was flying to the rescue. The bell was next to the stable. As the pig swooped overhead, he watched the other farm animals running into the barn. The birds and pig flew into the hayloft.

"Super Pork here to root out trouble!" Mort announced himself. "Is a flood coming? Is a kitten stuck in a tree? Is there a fuzzy monster attacking?"

"I'm afraid this is not a job for Super Pork," said Star the horse. "I called everyone here for a special meeting."

The horse neighed sadly then continued, "I've just learned that the farm is running out of money. If the farmer can't pay off his loan by the end of next month, he'll have to sell the farm. The bank wants to turn the farm into a new shopping mall."

"Who's going to want to shop at a mall full of farm animals?" asked a goose.

"It's all Mort's fault" barked Herb the dog. "He eats like a pig."

"Well, Star eats like a horse!" chirped one of the birds. Mort was their hero.

"I think the farmer's getting fleeced!" complained a sheep.

"Let's not start pointing wings, hooves, or paws," said Barb the cow. "We're all milking the farm dry."

"All I know is that we get by on chicken feed," cackled a hen.

Burt the Bull stood up. "Barb is right. We've got to come up with a solution."

"Can I speak?" asked Pepper the parrot.

"Of course you can," said Star. "Parrots are known for their ability to speak."

"Thank you," said Pepper. "As you know I am a house animal. So, I know what the farmer has been trying to do. He's been sending out lots of letters trying to get more money for the farm. He's applied for grants."

"Is that something we can eat?" asked Kirk the goat.

"Maybe you can," said Pepper, "but the rest of us can't. A grant is money people or governments give for a very specific reason. The farmer hopes to get a grant to turn the farm into a petting zoo."

"Kids with sticky hands petting us?" cried a sheep. "My cousin lived in a petting zoo and he once got a lollypop stuck in his wool. This is terrible."

"It's not the best solution," said the parrot, "but it's better than all of us getting sold off."

The animals all nodded in agreement. They didn't always get along, but deep down they all cared about each other, especially when Mort's pen was downwind.

"Why don't we apply for grants?" suggested Mort. "Maybe one of us will get money to help the farm?"

The animals agreed that was a great idea. They all decided to head down to the library to do some research on the internet. Soon they were all printing off forms and filling out paper work. Next, the animals marched down to the post office and mailed their grant applications.

The animals waited by the mailbox everyday expecting to hear good news about their grant. Two weeks passed and things were getting more hopeless. Each day fewer animals showed up at the mail box until finally only Mort and his birds waited.

It was a good thing, too. One day, the mailman delivered a large brown envelope. It was addressed to Mortimer Pig. The pig squealed with delight as he trotted back to the barnyard. The birds flew ahead and started ringing the bell.

The excited farm animals gathered around as Mort opened the envelope. "It's a grant! The farm is saved," Mortimer squealed with delight as he handed the letter to Star.

All the animals cheered. All the animals cheered except one. The horse was reading the grant letter. Star neighed sadly.

"This grant won't save the farm," said Star. "Mort, you checked the Super Hero box, not the Farm box on the application. You have a Super Hero grant. You can only spend the money on super hero gadgets."

All the animals sighed and sadly walked away. They were all so disappointed in Mort. The pig slumped in the dirt.

The birds were still excited, "What can we do with all this money?"

"Do whatever you want with it," said Mort. "If it won't save the farm, I don't care."

"Yippee!" chirped the birds.

A week later a large freight truck rumbled down the driveway. The little birds directed it to the back of the farm. Several very large crates were unloaded. The birds set up a tent to keep their work secret. They then began their mysterious work.

A few days later the birds fluttered around Mort's pen. The pig was still wallowing in mud and sorrow. All the farm animals were still upset with him about the super hero grant. The animals were running out of time to save the farm.

"Come to the fort, Mort," chirped the birds.

The birds lived in a tree house fort. They helped Mort put on his Super Pork shirt and cape. The birds flew him to their tree. The pig was surprised when he landed in the fort. The birds had transformed their little tree house into a high-tech communications center.

"What is this?" asked the bewildered pig.

"We used the super hero grant money," explained a bird.

"We installed a Big Bad Wolf Monitoring Service," explained another bird. "We'll make money to save the farm."

"How?" asked Mort.

"Our customers pay Super Pork to chase off big bad wolves. So far, we've signed up three little pigs and maybe soon Little Red Riding Hood," explained the bird.

"Wow, they're famous," said Mort. "But, they live far away. How could I get there in time to save them from big bad wolves? Some of those wolves are pretty quick."

"Can I, can I?" one of the birds hopped up and down.

"Yes," said the other birds.

The bird jumped onto a red button. The floor of the tree house slid open. Mort yelled as he started falling toward the ground. Suddenly the ground opened up. Mort landed on a soft seat.

Now the pig was moving up. A large machine rose from the ground. It was sleek and shiny. The pig was amazed.

"What is it?" asked Mort.

"It's the Porkmobile, a supercharged jet engine tractor," explained a bird.

Chapter 2

The Second Little Pig

Suddenly an alarm sounded. A bird fluttered out of the tree house.

"A big, bad wolf has been spotted. He's nearing the first little pig's house!" chirped the bird that had monitoring duty.

"It's a good thing you're already in the driver's seat Super Pork," said a bird.

"I don't know how to drive a Porkmobile," said Mort. "I don't even know how to drive a bicycle."

The birds were busy strapping themselves into little chairs at the top of the windshield. They put on tiny helmets. Super Pork found his helmet and strapped it on, too.

"Don't worry," said the bird at the top center of the windshield. "Leave the flying to us like always. We're experts."

"Fly?" gulped Super Pork.

The bird had its own steering wheel and control panel. It reached out a wing and pushed a button. The jet engine roared to life. The tractor rose slightly off the ground. The tires folded sideways like wings. Whoosh!

In a flash they were at the first little pig's house. The wheels flipped down and the tractor rested on the ground. The birds hopped from their seats. They unlatched Super Pork from his seat. The pig was still woozy from the ride.

"Go get the big, bad wolf Super Pork!" chirped the birds.

The frightened pig peered through his window. The big, bad wolf was coming up the sidewalk toward the first little pig's house of straw. Mort tried to walk, but his legs were still wobbly. He fell right over and landed on a lever.

Suddenly a compartment opened in the front of the tractor. A giant fly swatter popped out. Super Pork tried to get up, but kept falling over more levers. The fly swatter started moving.

Slap! Slap! Slap! The fly swatter hit the ground all around the big, bad wolf. The wolf twisted and dodged. Finally, it scampered away.

The birds cheered. Super Pork was a natural at using the Porkmobile. They didn't even know they had gotten the fly swatter option. The first little pig ran from the house to thank Super Pork. He was so grateful.

The birds strapped themselves into their seats. Super Pork was feeling very confident now. The pig turned the engine on low. He turned the steering wheel and headed the tractor for home. He wanted to show the pigs he could do it by himself.

When he saw all the birds were strapped in he pushed the green go button in front of him.

"No!" chirped a bird.

But it was too late. Fire shot from the back of the jet engine. The first little pig's house burst into flames. The pig grabbed a fire extinguisher and was trying to put it out. It was too late. The house was gone. The sad little pig scampered off to the second little pig's house.

The jet tractor shot into the sky. In no time, they were back at the tree house. Super Pork was glad they were successful at chasing away the big, bad wolf. Nevertheless, it was upsetting that he had totally destroyed the first little pig's house.

"It's ok," comforted one of the birds. "Straw is a renewable resource."

"There's no time to be upset," said the dispatcher bird. "There's just been another big, bad wolf sighting. This time, he's heading toward the second little pig's house."

The birds and Super Pork took their positions on the Porkmobile supercharged jet engine tractor. The bird captain launched the rocket engine. Zoom! They were off and they didn't even catch anything on fire.

Soon they arrived at the second little pig's house. It was a glass dome. Mort was relieved. It was completely fire proof. The first and second little pigs stared out the window. They were very frightened. The big, bad wolf was just about to cross the road to the second little pig's house.

Super Pork decided to honk at the wolf to scare him. He reached for the bright, blue button on the center of the steering wheel. The bird captain saw what was about to happen. He started to chirp, but it was too late.

The button wasn't the horn. It was the sonic boom power take-off. With a loud noise, rockets shot off under the tractor. It went straight up, faster than the speed of sound. A sonic boom followed.

Super Pork and the birds watched from the sky as cracks formed all over the doom. The big, bad wolf ran into the woods. The two little pigs scampered out of the house. The pigs made it just in time as the dome glass house shattered into millions of pieces. The pigs ran to the third little pig's house.

Mort sighed. The birds sighed too. Although they had thwarted another big, bad wolf attack, Super Pork and crew were somewhat upset about destroying two pig homes in one day. They were very tired and sad. Fortunately for everyone, the big, bad wolf was a little rattled too. He took the rest of the day off.

That night, Mort took the Porkmobile operator's manual home with him. He studied and studied. By the next morning he was already half-way through the book. He learned when to and not to fire the jet engines. He learned when to and not to use the sonic boom take-off.

The next morning, another truck rumbled through the farm. It drove up to the bird's tree house and left another large crate. Mort couldn't wait to see what it was. He ran after the truck.

By the time Mort reached the crate, the birds were already prying boards loose. It was an option for the Porkmobile, one of the birds explained. It had been on backorder. Inside the box were a several bags of grain and a strange looking machine.

"What is it?" asked Mort.

"It's a corn planter attachment for the Porkmobile," explained a bird. "We can plant an entire field in just seconds. We can grow corn to save the farm. It's a good thing too. We've had a hard time getting new pigs to sign up for the big, bad wolf monitoring service for some reason."

"I'm just glad we signed the third little pig to a one year contract," said another bird. "He tried to cancel out this morning."

The birds hooked the planter up to the Porkmobile. They filled the little grain bins on the planter with seed corn. Mort watched. He was a little sad. The birds were trying so hard, but they didn't realize it was too late to plant corn for the year.

The birds hopped in their little seats. They motioned for Mort to join them. The pig took his place behind the big steering wheel. The bird started the engine. The tractor rose from the ground. The wheels folded under. They steered the tractor toward the field.

The bird pushed the corn planting button. Suddenly they all wished they had read the operator's manual for the corn planter. The Porkmobile with the planter attached was spinning out of control. Corn was flying all over the field.

Chapter 3

Huff and Puff

"Must…touch…that…button," strained the bird that was piloting the Porkmobile.

Finally, the bird was able to extend its wing just enough to hit the button. The spinning slowed down. The tractor rested gently in the field. The birds and pig staggered wildly back to the tree house.

"Call the Porkmobile 1-800 number," the captain bird told the dispatcher bird. "We need to find out what happened."

The dispatcher bird put the call through. The only problem was that it tied up the line for the big, bad wolf monitoring system alarm. The captain bird was on hold for over twenty minutes. Finally he got through to the technical help line.

"Oh, I see," the bird spoke into the phone. "I should have known better."

The bird felt a little foolish. It had forgotten to flip the switch from rescue mode to farm mode. The poor Porkmobile on-board computer system couldn't decide whether to plant the corn or rescue the corn. The bird thanked the technician and hung up.

As soon as the bird hung up the phone, the big, bad wolf alarm started to sound.

"Oh no," groaned the dispatcher. "The big, bad wolf alarm code couldn't get through while you were on the phone. The big, bad wolf went to the third little pig's house over twenty minutes ago."

"We've got to get call waiting," sighed a bird.

"There's no time to waste," said Super Pork. "To the Porkmobile!"

In a few minutes, they were on their way to the third little pig's house. When they landed, they didn't like what they saw. The third little pig lived in a steel two-story house. The front door was wide open. The big, bad wolf was no where in sight outside.

The pig and the birds rushed inside the house. They were shocked at what they saw next. The big, bad wolf was relaxing at the dinner table. He was sipping a cup of coffee. In front of him was a plate with just a few crumbs on it.

"Are those pig crumbs?" whispered a bird.

Suddenly, the three little pigs burst through the kitchen door.

"We saw you land and wanted to bring you some cookies," said the third little pig.

"They're really good," said the big, bad wolf. "They're cut-out cookies shaped like little pigs with pink icing, my favorite."

The birds and Super Pork just stared in disbelief. Each of the three little pigs picked up a pen and scribbled on some papers. The third little pig gathered them up and handed the papers to the big, bad wolf. He scanned them quickly.

"It looks like everything is in order," said the wolf. "Congratulations!" He reached out his paw and shook their hooves. Then he looked at the birds and Super Pork. "Now if you will excuse me, I must get going. I took the afternoon off yesterday and fell behind on my appointments. It's over the hills and through the woods to Grandmother's house I go."

The wolf left the house and closed the door behind him. The birds and Super Pork were shocked.

"We got the big, bad wolf alarm and came to your rescue," Super Pork tried to explain, "but why did you let him in."

The third little pig giggled, "It turns out the wolf was selling insurance. With all the problems my brothers have had, I thought insurance was a good idea."

"You bought insurance from a wolf?" asked a bird.

"Yes, my brothers and I each bought life insurance. I also bought home owner's insurance. I got the multi-line discount."

"Why did you buy life insurance from a wolf?" asked Super Pork.

"Who better to buy life insurance from? He won't eat us if he has to pay our relatives a huge amount of money," explained the first pig.

"That's right," agreed the second pig. "That thought alone takes away his appetite."

"We made sure we got the Consumed by Wolf coverage," the first little pig added. "It helps us all out. If the big, bad wolf can afford to eat at nice restaurants, he won't go door to door looking for food."

"Well I guess our work is done here birds," said Super Pork.

The birds and Super Pork climbed onto the Porkmobile. Just as they were getting ready to take off, a sharp object poked Super Pork on the shoulder. Mort turned around and almost jumped off the tractor in fright. It was the big, bad wolf poking him with a claw.

"I forgot to give you my card," said the wolf.

He handed Super Pork a card. Mort read it: Huff and Puff Insurance, Big Bad Wolf, Saleswolf.

"I've got to rush now," said the wolf. "But, call me."

The wolf forgot about the planter. He tripped over it. Big Bad landed right on a bright orange button. The corn planter started to hum. Then, it started to glow. Suddenly beams of light shot out the back.

The beams swept back and forth hitting the third little pig's house. As the ray beam struck the walls, they started disappearing. Soon, nothing was left except the three little pigs sitting at the kitchen table.

"There it is," said the third little pig as it pointed to a piece of paper. "I'm glad I bought the Super Hero Damage Coverage. House disintegration, it's right here in my policy."

The big, bad wolf was crying as he scampered off to Red Riding Hood's grandmother's house, "My boss is going to hate me."

Super Pork and the birds were excited when they got back to the tree house. It was the first time *they* didn't destroy a pig's house. The dispatcher bird wanted to hear all about it.

Super Pork told the story as they all gathered around the Porkmobile, "…and the wolf fell right on the orange button like this!" the pig pushed the button.

"No!" shouted the bird captain. But, it was too late.

The planter began to hum. Then it began to glow. Suddenly ray beams shot all over the freshly planted corn field. Mort was afraid the ground was going to disappear. The beams stopped after a few minutes.

"We didn't fully charge the ray beam batteries before use," said a bird who was studying the corn planter's owner's manual.

"It's a good thing, too," said Super Pork. "The ray beam didn't do anything to the field.

But, Super Pork was wrong. The next morning, all the animals gathered around Mort's pen. When they all let off a cheer, the pig jumped up out of a sound sleep. He didn't know what happened, but everyone looked happy.

"You did it Mort!" said Star the horse.

"You saved the farm," cried Spunky the puppy.

"Your super hero grant was just what we needed," added Burt the Bull.

They led him out to the cornfield. It looked different than the night before. The bare, freshly planted ground was now filled with corn stalks. They were each about thirty feet high. On each corn stalk were ears of corn over six feet long.

"The switch was in farm mode," a bird explained to Mort. "Your knee must have bumped it when you got off the Porkmobile. When you pushed the orange button, it activated the super corn growth ray."

"The farmer has bushels of corn to sell now," explained Star. "We're rich. The farm is saved. You are Super Pork!"

All the animals cheered in agreement.

Manimator

Story and illustrations by
Brian Davis

When a little drawing named Zeroy hears for the first time, his understanding of his world completely changes. Sharing the truth with his friends becomes a difficult challenge, especially when a new arrival invades Eepland.

Vocabulary Words

animator
bicker
exhausted
fabulous
frustrated
interrupted
lurking
revelation
slither
theory

Chapter 1

Eeple Ears

Zeroy was woken up by a noise.

"A noise? What's a noise?"

It was the first sound Zeroy had heard since he had been drawn. Little Zeroy was one of the first Eeples drawn by the animator. Eepland was the animator's special project.

"See Daddy, I'm a manimator just like you!" said a high pitched voice.

"Manimator? What's a manimator?" thought Zeroy to himself. In fact, he thought so hard he didn't hear the man correct the little girl.

"That's animator, Tiffany," said the father's voice.

"Manimator!" Tiffany repeated.

"Manimator, there's that word again," Zeroy had heard Tiffany.

"Tiffany, I told you not to draw on that paper." said the girl's father.

"But, you didn't put ears on the Eeples. See, I put two ears on Zeroy. I'm a manimator like you." said the little girl.

"Zeroy!" thought the little drawing. "They're talking about me! What's talking?" Zeroy was once again lost in his thoughts.

The little girl's father explained to her that Eeples don't have ears. They don't even need ears. There are no sounds in Eepland. Eeples think to one another.

When the little girl spoke again Zeroy was listening. "I'm glad you're a manimator. I like Eepland a lot. You draw very well Daddy."

"I like drawing eeples," answered the father as he hugged his little girl.

"Draw! Eeples!" thought Zeroy excitedly. "The manimator drew...me!" Zeroy bounced up and down, he was so happy. "I was drawn by the manimator, I was drawn by the manimator..." Zeroy sang his new found revelation over and over again. Exhausted, the little drawing lay down and thought, "What's a Manimator?"

Zeroy sat up and pressed his nose to the paper. He tried so hard to look out, but all he could see was the flat world of paper all around him.

"Tell me about Eepland again, Daddy!" pleaded Tiffany. Her father sat the little girl on his knee.

"When I finish Eepland it will have..." The animator told the little girl all his wonderful plans for his special little world.

Zeroy sat and listened. The little drawing giggled and smiled as he heard his Manimator reveal the plan for Eepland. When the father was finished, Zeroy heard his creator send the little girl off for bed.

The girl's father looked at Zeroy and laughed a happy laugh. "Eeples don't have ears," was the last thing Zeroy heard. The animator brushed off the eraser rubbings that carried away the two tiny marks that had been Zeroy's ears. The little drawing felt the sides of his head where the ears had been.

"Easy come, easy go," he thought.

The animator stretched and yawned.

"Meow" a cat said as it walked through the doorway.

"Hi Boots," said the man as he picked up the cat. "What do you think of Eepland?"

The cat purred its approval.

"I agree," said the animator. The man gently set the cat down. He put his pencil on the drawing pad and turned out the light. "I'll work on it some more in the morning."

After the man had left, Boots the cat hopped up on the drawing pad. The cat accidentally stepped on a small glob of red paint. Boots didn't notice the paint until he took a step. The paint left a red paw print on Eepland. The cat quickly licked the paint from his foot and left the room.

The room was now dark and quiet. Everything was still, everything except Eepland. There was no nighttime in Eepland. The page was always white. To the eeples, Eepland was a vast, unexplored area. They had never traveled its undrawn areas. They had never ventured to the edges of the pad.

There were many theories about those uncharted areas. There were also exciting stories, stories about eeple eating scribble monsters. Most eeples believed that if you were to walk in one direction you would eventually circle Eepland and come back from the other direction. This was commonly known as the Circular Eepland theory.

Zeroy climbed up some scribbles to a box that was being drawn as his house. He peered over Eepland. He tried to imagine all the Manimator's plans.

"It will be so beautiful!" Zeroy thought to himself. He couldn't wait to tell the other eeples. Zeroy spotted his first chance to spread the message.

Dowtle and Vainilla were sliding down some curves a few scribbles above him.

"Hey Eeps!" Zeroy thought to them.

"Did someone just think to us?" Vainilla thought to Dowtle.

"I don't think so," Dowtle thought back. Zeroy, realizing he was out of thinking distance began to climb up some shapes. He slipped once or twice on a circle.

"Curves are tricky," he thought to himself. As he got close to the other two he thought out to Dowtle, "Can you help me up?"

"Probably not," Dowtle thought back, but he stretched out his hand anyway.

Dowtle was able to pull Zeroy up enough for Zeroy to get a good grip on the line. He then pulled himself the rest of the way up. He stood up and started to walk toward the two eeples. He didn't notice the hand that was reaching up from the other side of the box. The hand grabbed his ankle. Zeroy tripped and rolled down one curve then another until he landed face first on a large, hard, rectangle.

Zeroy rolled over and stared up the page. Above him Dowtle and Vainilla had been joined by a third eeple.

"I should have known it was you Meenee." Zeroy thought angrily.

"Did you have a good trip?" Meenee thought back.

Zeroy was about ready to think something really bad when Evey and Seebee walked up.

"What happened?" thought Evey to Zeroy. Then she noticed Meenee laughing above them.

"Oh, it's Meenee again," she thought.

Dowtle and Vainilla slid down the curves. Meenee, realizing he was alone, started to follow them. As he approached the curve, he tripped over his own feet and rolled down the curve. Meenee rolled over Vainilla at the bottom of the curve. He was half dazed when Vainilla came over and started kicking him.

"I can't believe you messed up my beautiful hair!"

The eeples laughed as Zeroy pulled her away.

Chapter 2

What's a Manimator

When they had all settled down, Zeroy began to think to them. "I woke up earlier and I had ears..." his thoughts were interrupted by the other eeples.

"Ears? What are ears?" they all thought to Zeroy.

"Well, they are lines of course. Curvy lines on my head." The eeples started searching Zeroy's head, looking for the mysterious ears.

"I don't see any ears," Seebee observed.

"I don't think he ever had ears," thought Dowtle.

"And even if he did. I would still be prettier," added Vainilla.

Evey stared angrily at Meenee.

"I didn't take them!" thought Meenee.

Zeroy brushed away their hands. "I had ears, but they're gone now. The Manimator took them."

"See, I told you I didn't take his ears!" thought Meenee.

Before Zeroy could begin his explanation he was interrupted again.

"What's a Manimator?" they all thought.

"He's...well he's..." Zeroy realized he didn't have a good explanation.

"What does he look like?" thought Seebee.

"I don't see him, I heard him!" Zeroy was starting to get frustrated.

"Heard, what's heard?" all the eeples thought to Zeroy.

"Oh!" groaned Zeroy in his thoughts. The more he explained, the more he needed to explain.

"Heard is what I did with my ears."

Evey's thoughts interrupted again, "Is heard the place where eeples lose their ears? Is it..." she thought in almost a whisper as the other eeples waited wide-eyed for her question. "Is it in the undrawn area?"

“Oooh!” the eeples shuddered at the thought.

“No...” Zeroy finally had their attention, “heard is what happens when you know the Manimator’s thoughts.”

The relieved eeples all let out the breath they had been holding.

“Finally, I’m making some progress,” Zeroy thought to himself.

“I don’t think there is a Manimator,” thought Dowtle.

“I’ve never seen the Manimator,” added Seebee.

“I wouldn’t let some Manimator take my ears!” Meenee added.

“You don’t have ears. Eeples don’t have ears. If they did, mine would be the prettiest,” added Vainilla.

“I doubt that,” Dowtle thought back.

“You doubt everything!” said Evey.

The eeples bickered back and forth. They fought over who would have the prettiest ears, if eeples had ears. They fought over who was the bravest, and they dared each other to go to Heard, which was of course the place where all the eeples ears were kept. The thoughts were flying so fiercely that no one noticed the sad little drawing slide off the rectangle and walk away.

Zeroy was discouraged. He didn’t get to tell them of the wonderful plans that the Manimator had for Eepland. They didn’t know the wonderful truth that the Manimator drew them.

“Manimator! Manimator!” Zeroy thought out his creator’s name, hoping for a thought in return.

If Zeroy’s head hadn’t been so low, if he hadn’t been so absorbed in his thoughts, he would have noticed something very unusual in Eepland. He was being spied on by something lurking behind a triangle.

The glob of red paint watched Zeroy walk away.

“Manimator, Manimator,” grumbled the red glob to itself. “The Manimator never uses enough red. I don’t like the Manimator.”

The glob slithered over toward the arguing Eeples. He hid behind a triangle and listened with delight. He laughed at the Manimator’s creation.

"So these are the silly little creatures he's so crazy about. They're all the Manimator talks about. He never talks about red!" The red glob began to pout as he watched the eeples.

"Hmmmph! They don't even have a solid color. They're lines, that's all they are! They aren't red. I am." The glob took great delight in being red. Beauty, perfection, and red, they were all the same to the glob.

The glob kept mumbling. It kept getting angrier. This was nothing unusual for the red paint. No matter what the Manimator drew, the glob never felt he used enough red. "If I were the Manimator, everything would be red!" he thought to himself.

The red glob knew very well that it could never be the Manimator. It knew that a brush needed the hand of the Manimator to create.

"If the Manimator would give up on this senseless plan for Eepland, maybe he would paint Redland." Redland had always been the glob's dream.

The glob shaped itself into an evil smile. The glob had a plan. "What if the eeples destroyed Eepland? The Manimator would be so discouraged. Then, he would be ready to draw Redland. This should be easy with these simple line drawings," it thought as it watched the bickering eeples.

The eeples were still arguing when the red glob slithered up to them. They never noticed it. The red glob thought loud thoughts. Still, no one paid attention. It shaped itself into ferocious looking globs. No one noticed.

It was accidentally knocked off the triangle. No one noticed. Finally, the red glob zig zagged between their legs and tripped them all.

"Oops, I didn't see you there!" lied the glob.

"What are you?" thought Evey. "Are you the Manimator?" thought Seebee.

"Hmmm...this could be real easy," thought the glob.

Just when the glob was about to answer yes, Dowtle thought, "It's not the Manimator." "You're right, I don't see any ears," agreed Seebee.

"If it had ears, I would still be prettier," added Vainilla.

"You would not!" screamed the red paint. "I am red!"

Vainilla lifted her nose in the air and ignored the globs thoughts.

"Do you have to think so loud?" complained Meenee.

"What is red?" thought Evey.

"I am red," the glob answered proudly.

Chapter 3

The Great Number 2

"See, I told you he wasn't the Manimator," thought Dowtle.

Deception had never been so difficult for the red glob. All of a sudden it was being backed into a corner. These little creatures were making it necessary for him to tell the truth, at least part of it anyway.

"My name is Inkydoo," the glob began to explain. "I am better than the Manimator. For as you can see, I am red."

"What is red?" thought all the eeples at once.

Inkydoo was more than happy to explain. "Red is beauty. Red is true art. Red is what everything wants to be, and it's what I am."

"Wow," the Eeples sighed in awe as they stared at Inkydoo. The red glob drank in their adoration.

"Boots!" said the animator the next morning as he stared at Eepland. "I'll just have to wipe it off." He picked up a rag. "I have more problems with red paint," the animator muttered.

Inkydoo dug into the paper. It anchored itself to the fibers. "Oh! Ow! Stop! Stop!" It screamed as it ducked away from the rag. Inkydoo spread itself thinner and thinner until it became a big red smudge.

"I guess I'll just have to paint over it with white," muttered the animator. Just then, a phone rang. The animator turned off the light and left the room.

In the darkness, Inkydoo began to pull himself together.

"Paint over!" shuddered the red blob in fear and anger. "I've got to work fast! I've got to work fast!" Inkydoo often repeated himself when he was afraid, "Find the eeples, find the eeples..."

All the eeples had gone to their original places when the animator came into the room earlier. When the lights went out, they had all gathered to hear Zeroy tell about the Manimator. Zeroy stood behind a rectangle that came up to his elbows. The other eeples sat on a low rectangles facing him.

Zeroy had more success than the day before. He was able to explain all he knew about the Manimator. "...and we were all drawn by the Manimator." stated Zeroy as Inkydoo slithered behind the rectangles the other five eeples were sitting on.

Inkydoo whispered a thought to Dowtle. "He's making this up. I'm not going to believe it." The thought was so quiet Dowtle thought it was his own doubt.

To Vainilla he whispered, "How could anyone draw something as beautiful as me!" She too believed it was her own thought.

Next was Meenee. "This sounds too sweet and nice to be true." The red blob whispered a thought.

"I'll believe it when I see it," was the thought Inkydoo whispered as a thought to Seebee, before he slithered up behind Evey. Evey stood up and hugged Zeroy before Inkydoo was able to deceive her.

"I believe you, Zeroy," Evey thought to Zeroy. "I believe in the Manimator." Zeroy smiled.

"We don't believe you!" stated Dowtle angrily. "Let's go play something else."

Meenee, Dowtle, Vainilla, and Seebee turned and walked away.

"It's true. I'm not playing!" Zeroy thought loudly after them.

The four eeples hadn't gone far before Inkydoo oozed up to the top of a square in front of them.

"Ooo, it's that red thing," thought Vainilla disgustedly. She still believed she was prettier.

"You seem to be in a hurry," Inkydoo thought to them.

"We just want to get away from Zeroy and his silly Manimator stories," Seebee explained.

Inkydoo laughed, "They are quite silly aren't they! We all know the Manimator didn't draw the eeples. We all know how eeples were drawn, don't we?"

The eeples all nodded in agreement.

"This is so easy," Inkydoo thought to himself as he studied their blank faces.

"Well of course I know who drew the eeples, but the other three don't," thought Meenee arrogantly to Inkydoo.

"You don't know ei...ow...oh..." Meenee interrupted Dowtle's thought by stomping on his foot. Vainilla and Seebee knew they would be next if they said anything. "Would you please tell them?" thought Meenee politely to Inkydoo.

"Oh, I do enjoy the story," answered Inkydoo with a smile. "As we all know," he began," or at least as Meenee knows," Meenee nodded and smiled, then Inkydoo continued, "the eeples were drawn by the Great Number 2."

"The Great Number 2!" gasped the eeples.

"The Great Number 2," Inkydoo thought on as the eeples crowded up to him not wanting to miss a thought, "is a pencil."

"A pencil, that's what the Great Number 2 is," thought Meenee pridefully in agreement.

"I've never seen a pencil," thought Seebee.

"I don't even know what a pencil is," Dowtle thought to Inkydoo.

"I'll let Meenee tell you," thought Inkydoo to the eeples. The three eeples gathered around Meenee as Inkydoo stood behind them. "It's like..." Meenee was stammering, just waiting for the next thought, when he noticed Inkydoo pointing to a rectangle. "It's like a rectangle." Inkydoo pushed a triangle in front of it, "and it has an end like a triangle."

"What's so great about that? I don't believe you," thought Dowtle to Meenee.

"I don't see how a triangle and a rectangle could make an eeple" added Seebee. "Especially one as beautiful as me," thought Vainilla.

Inkydoo popped up in front of them. "A pencil makes eeples when it draws. But, if you don't believe me you don't need to go with Meenee and me to see the Great Number 2," Meenee nodded and smiled as Inkydoo put a tentacle-like arm on Meenee's shoulder and continued, "in the undrawn area!"

Chapter 4

The Undrawn Area

A look of terror spread on the faces of the eeples, especially Meenee. "I don't think I want to..."

Meenee tried to pull away from Inkydoo, but the red blob covered Meenee's mouth and gripped him tightly.

"Of course you don't want to share the Great Number 2 with everyone, but they deserve to see your fabulous maker. They have a right!"

"We have a right!" Dowtle, Seebee, and Vainilla all thought to Meenee angrily.

Meenee was only trying to back out before, but now he was angry at the other eeples.

"Okay, but don't expect me to bring you back if you get scared along the way." Meenee tried to act tough although he was terrified of going into the undrawn areas.

Inkydoo led the pilgrimage. The eeples with Meenee in front followed closely. They were at the same time excited and afraid. They didn't know what lay ahead of them in the undrawn area.

Soon they passed the outer edges of Eepland. The last rectangles seemed too safe and inviting. The pad ahead of them grew very unfamiliar, and very blank. What they didn't realize was that Inkydoo was purposely making the journey seem longer.

After they were out of sight of Eepland, Inkydoo led them along a zig zagged, snaking, winding path. If the eeples suspected anything, they didn't dare question Inkydoo. They were totally at his mercy. Unfortunately, they had no idea of how little mercy he had.

Back in Eepland, Zeroy and Evey were looking for their friends. After walking all around Eepland thinking out their names, the two eeples were growing more concerned.

“I don’t like this,” thought Zeroy.

“Me neither,” Evey thought back, “I don’t even see that creepy red blob.”

“I don’t trust that Inkydoo, whoever or whatever it is,” added Zeroy.

“I have an idea,” thought Evey as she started pushing a square up to a rectangle, “Let’s stack up some squares, climb up on top, and look for them.”

“That’s a great idea!” Zeroy answered as he began to help Evey with the square.

Soon they had made a tower of five squares. After climbing to the top they began to scan the pad. Not too far outside of Eepland, the eeples were following Inkydoo around in circles. Zeroy and Evey watched as the red blob led the other eeples toward a strange looking shadow.

“Everyone stay behind me,” Inkydoo cautioned. “We never know what kind of mood the Great Number 2 will be in.” Inkydoo approached the pencil alone. “I will tell you if it is safe,” he thought back to the eeples. The eeples huddled together and waited.

Eeples cannot see beyond the flat surface of their pad. The only part of an object they can see is the part touching the paper. If they could see beyond the pad they would have noticed that Inkydoo had a hold of the pencil lead. This allowed him to move the pencil.

“Would you grant your loyal subjects the pleasure of you presence?” Inkydoo pretended to ask the pencil. He shook the pencil slightly. “Eeples, you may pass under the Great Number 2,” invited the red blob.

The eeples slowly pushed Meenee toward the pencil. Meenee was more afraid of what the others would think of him than what the Great Number 2 could do to him. He finally stood up straight, and boldly approached the pencil. Inkydoo rocked the pencil slightly to greet Meenee. The other eeples jumped back a step.

Meenee reverently slid across the shadow of the pencil. Meenee drank in the color. He had never seen such a beautiful yellow before. He was in total awe when he saw the black lettering that read Number 2.

Meenee finished sliding under the pencil. As he walked around it to join the others, Inkydoo rocked the pencil gently in approval. Meenee no longer had to just act brave. He felt brave. The other eeples congratulated him as he rejoined them. Now the other three were eager to pass under the Great Number 2.

When the eeples returned to Eepland they were eager to share their new found wisdom with Zeroy and Evey.

"The Great Number 2 is...now I know this is hard to imagine, but the Great Number 2 is almost as beautiful as me," explained Vainilla.

"You've just got to see it," added Seebee.

"It's unbelievable," interrupted Dowtle.

"And I am not afraid of the Great Number 2," boasted Meenee.

All the while Inkydoo was thinking secret thoughts, silent thoughts that no eeple could hear. "It is now time for the next part of my plan. The eeples are now ready to destroy Eepland and the whole pad will me mine, mine, mine! The Manimator will be sorry he ever drew those miserable eeples."

"Time for class, my dear eeples," called out Inkydoo to his followers.

"Don't listen to it," warned Zeroy.

"The Manimator drew us, not the Great Number 2," added Evey.

Angrily Inkydoo turned back to them and snapped, "Have you ever seen the Manimator?" The prideful eeples blindly filed into a single line behind the red glob and marched off.

"Have you ever heard the Great Number 2?" countered Zeroy, but their minds were closed to the thought.

Chapter 5

Pencil Tops

Inkydoo's eager students sat on squares waiting for their red glob of a teacher to begin. Inkydoo started with the nature of the pencil. "You will notice that pencils are easily defined. They can be understood, unlike that silly concept of a Manimator. Who can tell me what shape is the Great Number 2?" They all raised their hands. Inkydoo called on Dowtle.

"I know that the Great Number 2 is a thin rectangle with a triangle on the end. You can only see the shadow of the triangle."

"Very good Dowtle, and you seemed so sure of yourself," complimented Inkydoo. Dowtle smiled and shook with delight.

"Now who can tell me what shape is the Manimator?" asked Inkydoo.

No one raised a hand, but they all giggled.

"Who can tell me what color is the Great Number 2?" continued the red glob.

"A beautiful yellow!" blurted out Vainilla.

"Very good, but next time wait for me to call on you," Inkydoo thought to her. The other eeples nodded in agreement. "I think I have made my point. Have I not? The Great Number 2 is real. The Manimator exists only in the mind of our dear, pitiful, friend Zeroy. Now we are ready to go on."

The eeples squirmed in their seats with excitement. Inkydoo leaned toward them and thought very quietly. The eeples leaned forward on the square. "You can be like the Great Number 2!"

The eeples fell backwards in shock. Inkydoo came even closer. "You can all be like pencils!" The red glob stopped to let it sink in. "I can help you find the pencil within yourself. For you see, there is not just one Great Number 2, but there are many! Everyone of you can be as great as the Great Number 2."

"Show us!" agreed the four eeples. Inkydoo pulled Meenee to the front.

"It's all up here," said the red glob pointing to Meenee's head. He reached up and carefully pulled out a long pointed object. The other eeples gasped in horror. Meenee almost fainted, but he knew he was too tough to faint.

"Now did that hurt?" asked Inkydoo.

"Not me," boasted Meenee.

"What do you think this is?" asked Inkydoo as he handed the rectangular object to Meenee.

"Why, it's a...it's a...pencil!" exclaimed Meenee.

Inkydoo spent the rest of the day helping the other eeples find their pencils. Then he introduced them to the power of drawing.

"What's the pink end of the pencil for?" asked Seebee. "That is another lesson. It will have to wait for another day. For now, class dismissed. Your homework is to go out and draw, draw, draw!"

The four eeples did just that. They drew on squares. They drew on rectangles. They drew on everything they could find. By the time Zeroy and Evey saw them Eepland was a mess.

"What have you done?" Zeroy thought to them in total shock. "Eepland looks awful," cried Evey.

"It's not!" argued Vainilla. "It's beautiful, like me."

Meenee giggled and pointed, "You look exactly like Eepland." Vainilla looked down at herself. Her arms, legs and clothes were scribbled on. She looked nothing like an eeple.

"I'll get you for this!" thought Vanilla angrily. She scribbled on Meenee. He tried to scribble back and made an ugly black mark on Dowtle. Seebee tried to step in to break it up and Vanilla scribbled on her face.

The four eeples rolled around scribbling on each other. Zeroy and Evey hopped up on a square to stay out of the way.

"This is terrible, just terrible!" thought Evey.

"Stop! stop!" Zeroy thought to the fighting eeples. By this time they were laughing at each other.

"Can't you see we're just playing?" thought Seebee.

"I can, but can't you see how you've made a mess of yourselves?" Zeroy answered.

"We can do what we want. We are like the Great Number 2. If we want to draw on ourselves, why do you care?" Dowtle asked.

"I care because the Manimator will care. He drew us. He has such wonderful plans for us. I'm sure he doesn't want you to make a mess of yourselves," Zeroy pleaded.

“We don’t believe in the Manimator. We are like pencils. We don’t even need a Manimator. We can draw.” thought Dowtle.

“But,” answered Evey, “Zeroy heard the Manimator with his own ears. He knows the Manimator is real, and I believe him!”

“He doesn’t have ears!” Dowtle pointed out.

An evil grin came on Meenee’s face as he grabbed Zeroy. “We could draw ears on him!” Vainilla and Seebee grabbed Evey. “She could use ears, too!”

Zeroy and Evey tried to get away, but it was no use. They were outnumbered and the pencils were too quick.

When the four eeples were done drawing ears, they left Zeroy and Evey and began scribbling on everything in Eepland, including each other.

“You have...ears!” Evey thought as she stared at Zeroy.

“So do you, Evey”

Evey jumped up, “What was that?” thought Evey.

“That was a...a...sound!” Zeroy excitedly answered in a whisper. They had heard a sound. Tiffany and her father were in the room.

“What happened to Eepland!” cried Tiffany.

“It’s ruined. I’ll have to start over,” groaned the Manimator.

“What about the eeples?” asked Tiffany.

Zeroy and Evey listened carefully. “They’ve all been scribbled on. I’ll have to throw them all away,” sighed the Manimator. Zeroy and Evey started jumping up and down. Suddenly Zeroy felt something strange in his throat. It was a voice. Zeroy could speak.

“No!” cried out the Eeple.

Zeroy’s voice wasn’t very loud, but it was loud enough to get Tiffany to look at the spot in Eepland that wasn’t totally scribbled on. “Look daddy! These eeples aren’t messed up.”

“You’re right,” agreed the Manimator. “They just need to be drawn again.”

Then Tiffany noticed the ears. “They have ears again. Can they keep them this time?” asked Tiffany.

The Manimator nodded and smiled, “I guess so, this time. We’ll start on New Eepland after breakfast.”

The Manimator did draw New Eepland. Because of their belief in the Manimator, Zeroy and Evey were the only two Eeples that were drawn again. They were also the first two Eeples in the New Eepland that the Manimator made it just for them.

Fabulous Fables

Stories and illustrations by
Brian Davis

The word *fable* comes from the Latin word *fabula*. It means "to speak a little story." Fables are short stories that teach a moral lesson. Many fables feature animals playing the roles of people.

The author of a fable is called a *fabulist*. The word fabulous originally meant "having to do with fables." Now it means wonderful.

The most famous fabulist was named *Aesop*. He was a Greek slave who lived around 550 B.C. Many of his stories have been retold by others.

The retelling of several of Aesop's fables can be found on the following pages.

Aesop public domain image

Vocabulary Words

anxiously	delicious	**fable**	recovery
apologize	delivery	**hyper**	reflection
candidate	**emperor**	**hypo**	**simulation**
complain	**examination**	magnifying	**truncated**
conflict	**expectation**	nervously	

Bold print words are the weekly vocabulary list used in the language workbook.

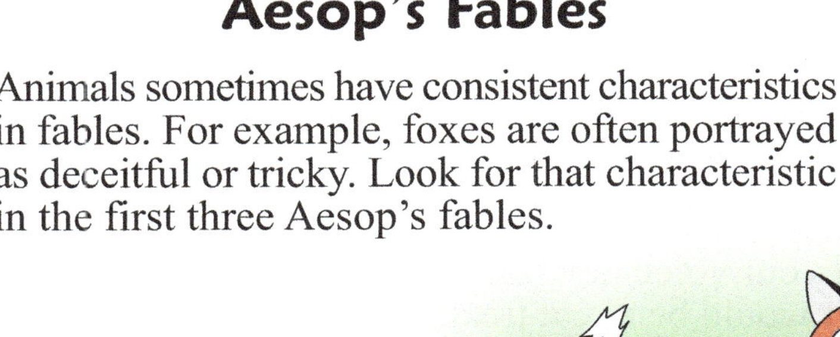

Aesop's Fables

Animals sometimes have consistent characteristics in fables. For example, foxes are often portrayed as deceitful or tricky. Look for that characteristic in the first three Aesop's fables.

Chapter 1

Fox Tales

The Fox and the Stork

A fox and a stork decided to be friends. The fox invited the stork for dinner. The fox made a delicious soup. The stork waited in eager expectation at the dinner table. The wonderful smell came from the kitchen. At last the fox stepped from the kitchen carrying two shallow bowls.

The fox quickly lapped his up. The stork could only get the tip of its beak wet.

"I see you really didn't enjoy the soup. I'll eat it for you," said the fox. He lapped up the stork's bowl of soup.

"I hope I did not offend you for not eating the soup," said the stork.

"Not at all," said the fox.

"Then join me at my house for dinner tomorrow," said the stork.

"I would be delighted," said the fox.

The next day, the fox came to the stork's house. The fox sat at the table hungrily awaiting the meal. The delightful smell came from the oven. At last the stork stepped from the kitchen. It carried two long-necked jars with wonderful chunks of fish in the bottom.

The stork skillfully picked chunk after chunk of fish up with its long beak. The fox licked at the top of the jar, but his tongue was too short to reach the delicious meal.

"I see you really don't enjoy fish," said the stork. "I'll be happy to eat it for you." At that, the stork snatched all the fish from the fox's jar and gulped it down.

One bad turn deserves another.

The Fox and the Crow

A fox was sniffing along when he caught a whiff of cheese. His nose led him right to the delicious morsel. Just as he was about to gulp it down, a crow swept in and snatched it in its beak. The fox followed the crow as it landed in a branch high above his head.

"Mrs. Crow," yelled the fox. "I find your voice delightful. Would you please sing me a song? I would enjoy it so much. It would be a real treat."

The crow was pleased that someone could enjoy her voice. She opened her beak and started singing. The cheese tumbled toward the ground. The fox caught it in the air and gulped it down. The fox smacked its lips and said, "Mrs. Crow, your singing was truly my treat."

Beware of false flattery.

The Donkey's Brain

A fox and lion went hunting together. Having very little luck, the fox devised a plan. "I will send a message to the donkey. I will propose a peace treaty between the donkey, you, and me. I will invite him to come to this spot."

So, the fox sent a message to the donkey. The donkey wanted to live in peace, so he gladly came. As soon as he arrived, the lion pounced from the bush. After a lengthy battle, the lion killed the donkey. By this time, the lion was too tired to eat.

"Don't even touch the donkey before I wake up," the lion warned the fox. "I shall pick my part first. You may have my leftovers."

The fox felt he was as deserving as the lion. It was his plan that brought the donkey to them. Still, he feared the lion.

The lion took a long nap. The fox didn't touch the donkey at first, but the temptation grew. So did his hunger. Finally, the fox could wait no longer. He broke open the donkey's skull and ate its brain.

A short time later the lion awoke. When he saw the donkey he was furious. "I told you not to touch the donkey! Now his brain is missing." The fox shook his head, "Lion, the donkey never had a brain. If he had, he wouldn't have fallen for my plan." The lion could not stop laughing.

A quick wit can turn away wrath.

The Greedy Dog

The butcher tossed the stray dog a meaty bone. As the dog trotted away he crossed over a bridge. The dog happened to glance down and saw his reflection in the river.

"What a fine looking dog," he thought. "I believe that bone is larger than the one in my mouth."

The dog snarled at the reflection. The reflection snarled back at the same time. At that, the dog attempted to snatch the bone right out of the reflection's mouth. With a great splash the dog's bone was lost forever.

Be careful not to lose what you have by chasing after an illusion.

The Town Mouse and the Country Mouse

There once was a town mouse who visited her cousin in the country. The country mouse was very happy to see her favorite cousin.

"Come and eat," said the country mouse. "I will serve you my finest."

She brought out some kernels of corn, a stale bread crust, and a scrap of cheese.

"How can you live with such plain food as this?" asked the town mouse. "Come with me and I'll give you a feast."

The mice arrived at the town mouse's home that evening. Sure enough, the owners of the home had left out a feast. There was fruit, cake, and smoked meat. The country mouse had never seen such fine food and in such great quantity.

The mice scurried around the dining room, nibbling one delight after another. Suddenly they heard yapping and the clicking of paws on the hardwood floor.

"Run!" shouted the town mouse.

The two mice scrambled to a hole in the wall.

"What was that?" asked the country mouse.

"Just the owner's dogs," said the town mouse.

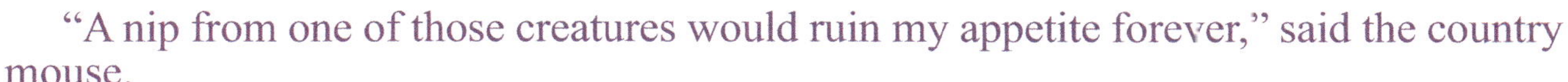

"A nip from one of those creatures would ruin my appetite forever," said the country mouse.

With that, the country mouse returned home, content to eat stale bread and cheese without fear.

Better a little with safety than much with no peace.

The Bat, the Birds, and the Beasts

The birds and the beasts got into a conflict over who had the right to a field. They marched to the battle field to settle the dispute. As the birds passed the bats they called out, "Come join us in battle to fight the beasts."

The bats answered, "We have no feathers, but fur. We are not birds, but beasts. We cannot join you." Later the beasts also passed the bats. They called out, "Come join us to battle the birds." The bats answered, "We have wings and fly. We are birds, not beasts. We will not be able to join you."

As the animals reached the field, they realized that they could share the field. The animals decided to live in peace. There was a great celebration in both camps. The bats asked the birds if they could join in the festivities. The birds answered, "You have no feathers. You are beasts." So the bats tried to join with the beasts. They too refused to let the bats join in. "You have wings and fly. You are not beasts."

He that is not one thing or another will have no friends.

Androcles and the Lion

Dogs chased a runaway slave named Androcles. He hid in a forest that was the home of a great lion. The dogs feared entering the forest because of the ferocious beast. While hiding in the woods, the slave heard the groaning and moaning of the lion. Suddenly, the lion stepped out of the bushes. He stared right into the eyes of Androcles.

The slave wanted to run, but he knew the dogs would be waiting. Then, he noticed that the lion was limping. Androcles carefully approached the lion. The look of anguish on the lion's face filled the slave's heart with compassion. The slave gently lifted the paw. He pulled out a large thorn. Androcles tore his shirt and wrapped the paw in the cloth so the wound would heal.

A short time later, the slave and the lion were both captured. Androcles was sentenced to be thrown to the lion. The great beast had been starved for several weeks so he would show no mercy.

The emperor and his court came to the arena to watch the deadly punishment. Androcles was led to the middle of the arena. A heavy gate was lifted. Out charged the starving lion. He rushed to Androcles with his terrible teeth showing.

Just as the lion was about the pounce, he recognized Androcles. The lion knocked him over and licked him like a happy puppy. Androcles couldn't help but laugh. The lion's tongue tickled. The emperor was curious so he had the guards bring Androcles to him. The slave explained all that had happened. The emperor was so impressed that he gave Androcles his freedom and released the lion back into the jungle.

The grateful are worthy of honor.

Play: The Donkey Ride

Characters:
Narrator, Aldo, Carlo, Old Man, Husband, Wife, Filipo, Villager 1, Villager 2

Narrator: Aldo, a poor farmer, would often take bags of grain to the market. He would sell grain in order to buy things he could not grow. He usually only took a small bag that he could easily carry. Today he is taking a large bag because he has lots of things to buy.

Carlo: The donkey is loaded, Father. Can I come with you today?

Aldo: Are your chores done?

Carlo: I knew you would ask. I woke up early and did them all.

Aldo: You are a smart boy. Yes, you may come with me.

Narrator: Aldo and his son, Carlo, started toward the town. Soon, they met an old man on the road.

Old Man: That is a fine looking donkey. He looks strong and healthy. Is there something wrong with him?

Aldo: There is nothing wrong with this donkey. I take good care of him.

Old Man: Then there must be something wrong with you. You walk when you could ride. You must be a foolish farmer.

Narrator: The old man walked on down the road. The farmer decided he did not want to look foolish to anyone else.

Aldo: The donkey is strong and my legs are tired. Perhaps I am being foolish.

Carlo: Maybe you should ride the donkey, Father. You work hard all the time. Why not rest as we travel to town?

Narrator: So, the farmer climbed onto the donkey's back. After awhile they saw a husband and his wife walking up the road toward them.

Wife: Look how loaded down that poor donkey is.

Husband: With the man and the grain it is carrying a heavy load.

Wife: It's cruel. Mr. Farmer, you should be ashamed of yourself!

Husband: You shouldn't make that poor beast carry both you and that sack of grain.

Aldo: Perhaps you are right. The donkey is strong, but perhaps he is carrying too great a burden.

Carlo: I'll carry the grain, father. It would be foolish of you to walk.

Narrator: So, the son took the bag of grain onto his shoulders. It was heavy, but he didn't complain. As they continued on their journey, next they met a young man named Filipo. He was a friend of Carlo.

Filipo: Hello Carlo. Where are you going?

Carlo: Father and I are going to town to sell this grain.

Filipo: Your father rides. You walk. I know you are a good son, but I think your father is being cruel. You have to carry the burden and don't get to ride. Is your donkey too weak to carry both of you?

Aldo: I am not a cruel father. My donkey is not weak. Climb onto the donkey's back Carlo. We'll ride together.

Carlo: I will carry the grain on my back as I ride. That should be fair to the donkey.

Narrator: Aldo, Carlo, and the grain rode on the back of the donkey. The farmer was right. The donkey was strong and didn't seem to mind the load. As they approached some villagers who were heading to the country for a picnic, they smiled and waved.

Villager 1: You should be ashamed of yourselves. You are abusing that donkey. He does all the work and you just smile and wave. You should be reported to the sheriff!

Narrator: The farmer and his son felt ashamed of themselves.

Aldo: Look at our poor donkey. How could we have put such a burden on him? What can we do to make it up to him?

Carlo: I know. We have treated him like a beast. Now, we should treat him like a king. We can take these logs by the side of the road. We can build him a chair and carry the donkey on our shoulders.

Aldo: That is the least we can do to make it up to the donkey.

Narrator: The farmer and his son built a donkey throne. They placed it on two logs to carry the donkey on their shoulders. They placed the bag of grain on the donkey's lap and continued on to the market.

Carlo: The load is heavy, but my heart is light. We are treating our donkey with kindness.

Aldo: Yes, you are right, son. We are nearing the village. Everyone will soon see that we are fair and kind.

Carlo: What is that crunching sound?

Aldo: It must be the gravel under our feet. We're not used to carrying a heavy load.

Narrator: The farmer and his son reached the village. As they walked to the market everyone stopped and stared. They had never seen such a sight. One by one the people at the market started laughing at the donkey riding like a king.

Carlo: Father, why are the people laughing at our kindness to the donkey?

Villager 2: We can't help but laugh. Why are two men carrying a donkey that is capable of carrying both of them? This is the most foolish thing we have ever seen.

Aldo: We are not foolish. We are kind.

Villager 2: You are foolish and kind. You were foolish when you carried the donkey. You were kind when you let the donkey eat all your grain.

Narrator: Sure enough, the donkey was crunching on the last bit of grain. Aldo and Carlo had nothing left to sell.

Aldo: If you try to please everyone, you will please no one.

Carlo: Except donkeys.

Fable: The Donkey Ride

A farmer decided to take some grain to the market. He loaded the sack on his donkey. The man and his son set out for town. As an old man met them, he commented about how foolish it was for the farmer to walk instead of riding the donkey. The farmer didn't want to look foolish, so he climbed onto the donkey's back.

A husband and wife passed them next. The wife commented about how cruel it was for the donkey to carry the man and the grain. So, the son carried the grain. Next, a younger man passed by and couldn't believe that the son had to walk and carry the entire burden. So the man and the son with the grain climbed onto the back of the donkey.

Some villagers passed next. They said they had never seen such cruelty shown to a donkey. The man and the son felt so awful. They decided to treat the donkey like a king. They built a royal platform and carried the donkey on their shoulders with the sack of grain on the donkey's lap.

The people in the market had never seen such a sight. They laughed at the silly farmer and his son. The farmer felt especially foolish when he discovered that the donkey had eaten all the grain.

If you try to please everyone, you will please no one.

The Elephant and Her Son

Chapter 1

Big Expectations

Mrs. Elephant was very excited when she found out she was going to be a mother. Mr. Elephant and she immediately began preparing for the big day. They only had twenty-two months before her big bundle of joy would arrive.

They shopped for little elephant clothes. The elephant couple bought an extra, heavy duty rocking chair. Mr. Elephant placed it in their new, baby elephant nursery. They even hung a little, pink elephant mobile over the crib. It turned gently while playing a happy lullaby.

One day, when Mr. Elephant was at work, he received a trumpet call. Mrs. Elephant was ready to go to Jungle General Hospital. They hurried so quickly that they arrived before the doctor. Mrs. Elephant was rushed to the delivery room. Mr. Elephant waited outside. The delivery room had a one elephant capacity.

Mr. Elephant paced nervously as he awaited the good news.

"Your first?" came a squeak near the elephant's ear.

The elephant looked up. On a shelf was a tiny waiting room. A mouse paced back and forth. He seemed as nervous as the elephant.

"Yes," answered the elephant. "Is it your first, too?"

"Yes," answered the mouse. "We've been waiting 22 days for this. It has seemed like forever. I thought this day would never come."

"We've waited 22 *months*," said the elephant. "We thought that was rushing it."

"My grandparents weren't even born 22 months ago!" exclaimed the mouse.

"You can come to the recovery room now," said a nurse.

"Me or him?" the elephant pointed to the mouse.

“Both of you,” said the nurse. “Your babies have been wheeled to the nursery. You may see them in a little while. You can see your wives now.”

Little did they know that moments earlier, two carts with two babies bumped each other in the hallway. The name cards fell onto the floor. The nurses picked them up and put them back on the carts. The mouse nursery became very crowded that day, and it only had one baby in it. There was plenty of room in the elephant nursery. That was unusual whenever there was even one elephant baby in the room.

Finally, the doctor arrived at the hospital.

“I’m sorry,” apologized Doctor Ape. “A vine broke on the skyway from my office. It caused quite a traffic jam. I had to swing all the way around the jungle.”

The doctor went room to room. He checked on Mrs. Elephant. He checked on Mrs. Mouse. Finally, he checked on the babies.

Mr. and Mrs. Elephant waited anxiously for the doctor to return. When he did, the doctor seemed upset. The elephants became more worried.

“Is our baby healthy?” asked Mrs. Elephant.

“Well,” sighed the doctor, “Perfectly healthy, but…”

“What?” asked Mr. Elephant.

“He’s a little bit on the small side,” the doctor explained. “A nurse is bringing him in.”

The nurse wheeled in the cart. The elephants peered in.

“Our baby is missing!” cried Mrs. Elephant.

Doctor Ape handed her a magnifying glass. He pointed to the little speck inside the blanket.

“There he is,” said Dr. Ape. “He is a bit on the small side; otherwise, he’s a very cute child. I’m sure he’ll have a growth spurt. Soon, he’ll be as big as the other elephants. Now, if you’ll excuse me, I must go talk to a couple of mice. They have a very big problem to deal with.”

“I’m not sure our baby clothes will fit him,” sighed Mr. Elephant.

The elephants tried to adjust. Mrs. Elephant cut the tags off the baby elephant clothes. She could make a whole outfit for her baby out of a single tag. They bought eyedroppers instead of baby bottles. They placed a matchbox inside the crib for their baby to sleep in.

In time, the baby grew; however, he didn’t grow very much. At first, they were hopeful. The baby grew so quickly. Then, after a few months, he stopped growing all together. Not only that, his trunk never formed. They took him to Dr. Ape.

“I’ve never seen an elephant stop growing at such a young age,” said Dr. Ape. “I see it with mice all the time, but never elephants. It could be worse.”

"Worse? How could it be worse?" asked Mr. Elephant.

"Well," said Dr. Ape, "I know a mouse family whose son hasn't stopped growing. He's huge! They're afraid he'll step on them and squish them. At least your son will never squish you."

"That is true," said Mr. Elephant. "I guess our problems could be bigger."

"What about his truncated trunk?" asked Mrs. Elephant.

"It looks like hypo-trunk-itis," said the doctor. "I'll have you see a specialist, Dr. Rhino. She's very good. I just referred a mouse family to her."

"A mouse can have hypo-trunk-itis?" asked Mr. Elephant.

"No, the mouse has hyper-trunk-itis. His nose is way too long. It's a very sad case. It's the only one I've ever seen," explained Dr. Ape.

Chapter 2

Dr. Rhino

The next day, Mrs. Elephant traveled through the jungle toward Dr. Rhino's office. Her son was tucked securely behind her ear. The doctor's office door opened as she arrived. A teary-eyed mouse sitting on the head of a young elephant stepped outside. Mrs. Elephant thought the young elephant was extremely adorable. She wondered how the mouse could be so sad.

The waiting room was very crowded. Mrs. Elephant watched as her son played with the other young animals. He started playing with some young mice. They seemed to accept him as one of their own.

"Come back here, son," whispered the elephant when she saw the mice. "We don't play with rodents."

"Yes, mother," answered her son, "but, I don't see anything wrong with them."

"They're dirty little animals," explained the elephant. She looked up at a shelf and saw the mother mouse give her an angry look. "No offense," the elephant apologized.

"Mrs. Elephant, Dr. Rhino will see you now," said a nurse.

Mrs. Elephant followed the nurse down a wide hallway. Inside was an elephant sized examination table. Mrs. Elephant lowered her trunk. Her son scampered down to the bed. A few minutes later, Dr. Rhino came in.

"Good morning," said Dr. Rhino as she flipped through a chart. "It looks like you are seeing me about hypo-trunk-itis."

"Yes," said Mrs. Elephant.

Dr. Rhino looked puzzled. "You have a very fine trunk. I see no problem."

"Not me," explained Mrs. Elephant. "It's my son."

"Then bring him right in," said Dr. Rhino.

"He is here sitting on the examination table."

"There is no elephant on my examination table," said Dr. Rhino. "Perhaps you need an eye doctor."

"He is there. See the tiny speck?" challenged the elephant.

Dr. Rhino turned on a light above the table. She grabbed a magnifying glass.

"Oh, there's the little fellow," said the rhino as she stared through the glass.

Suddenly, the rhino started sniffing. "What is that smell? It has a burnt fur smell to it."

"It's me!" cried the mouse. "The light through the magnifying glass is scorching my fur."

"Sorry!" apologized the doctor. "I've never seen such a tufted, tiny, trunkless elephant. This is amazing!"

"Can you help him out?" asked Mrs. Elephant.

The rhino tossed a glass of water onto the elephant's son.

"There, all put out. Just a little singed along the edges," said the doctor.

"Not that," said the elephant. "Can you cure him of hypo-trunk-itis?"

The rhino pulled up a computer. She snapped a picture with a camera that was hooked to the computer. The image of the elephant's son came up on the screen. The rhino tapped on the computer keys. She skillfully moved around the computer mouse and altered the picture.

"Now look at this," said Dr. Rhino. "Here is a computer simulation of your new son."

Mrs. Elephant looked hopefully at the computer screen as Dr. Rhino hit the enter key. The screen refreshed and slowly drew a trunk on the front of the picture.

"He's beautiful!" exclaimed the thrilled elephant before the picture could finish drawing.

Dr. Rhino was beaming too, until the picture finished drawing. That's when she noticed a problem. The picture now had a trunk, but the elephant's son's back feet were off the ground.

"The trunk would make your child too front heavy. He would always tip forward. I don't think he is a good candidate for a trunk transplant. I'm afraid there is no hope for your son."

Mrs. Elephant started sobbing. Dr. Rhino went to get a mop. Elephant tears are rather large. Puddles can form very quickly. Next thing you know, the smallest rodent patients would get washed right out the door.

The elephant's son was very sad too when they left. He wasn't disappointed about not having a trunk. He rather liked his nose. Still, he hated to see his mother so grieved.

As the elephant and her son traveled toward home, Mrs. Elephant wandered off the path. Her tear-filled eyes caused her vision to be blurry. Before she knew it she had wandered dangerously close to some hunters. In fact, she wandered right into their camp.

She was quickly surrounded by men with large guns. They were shouting directions to one another. They threw many ropes around her. She became tangled and confused. The men wrapped the ropes around some large trees. Mrs. Elephant had been captured.

Her son ran down her trunk. He charged at the men like he had seen other elephants do. He tried to knock the men over. They never noticed him.

The son ran off into the jungle. The mother watched him go. At first she was angry that her son would leave her alone with the humans. She grew sad when she realized how hopeless her situation was.

She strained against the ropes until she was too tired to fight. As she thought about her son, she realized how terrible she had been.

"It serves me right for my son to leave me. All I ever complained about were his imperfections."

Chapter 3

Just the Right Size

After a few hours of scampering across the jungle, the mouse reached home. His father was never happier to see him.

"Where is your mother?" asked the father.

"She has been captured by the humans. I tried to knock them over, but I just bounced off. We've got to help her."

Mr. Elephant gathered the other elephants around him. He told them about his wife's capture.

An old elephant stepped forward. "I have seen the men. They have powerful guns and they will be watching for us. We can't help your wife. You know the policy."

"I must go!" trumpeted the father elephant.

But, the other elephants closed around him. They wouldn't let him pass.

"If you go, you will be shot. We can't let that happen. It wouldn't bring Mrs. Elephant back to you."

"Please let me pass!" whaled Mr. Elephant.

There were too many elephants for Mr. Elephant to get by. They were all blocking his way. The elephants knew their friend would never stand a chance against the guns. They had seen it too many times.

No one noticed that the elephant's son had left. They couldn't have stopped him anyway. He could easily squeeze between their legs. The son was going back to his mother.

It was dark by the time the mouse reached the camp. His exhausted mother was asleep. All the fight had drained from her. Men with guns stood around the camp, ready to shoot any elephants that tried to rescue Mrs. Elephant. The son was surprised when they didn't notice him slip by them.

The son bounced up his mother's trunk.

"Wake up! Wake up!" squeaked the son.

His mother was too tired to hear the squeaks. The son jumped up and down on her head. He was too light. She didn't feel him through her tough skin.

The son was so angry and afraid that he bit into a rope. To his surprise, his sharp teeth slit right through the strands. The son continued gnawing. Soon, the first rope was completely cut.

The son gnawed throughout the night. One-by-one the ropes were cut. As the sun began to rise, the mother elephant yawned. She stretched her well-rested legs. In the haziness of sleep, she didn't realize where she was.

Then she remembered her captors. She looked around the camp. All the men with guns had drifted off to sleep. She started to strain against the ropes one more time.

Something strange happened. The ropes simply fell away. The elephant was surprised. Then, something caught her eye.

Something warmed her heart. There at her feet was her son. Even in his sleep her exhausted child was still gnawing at the ropes.

The mother elephant gently lifted him with her trunk. She placed him behind her big floppy ear. As quietly as an elephant can sneak, she slipped back into the jungle.

Before the sun had fully risen, Mrs. Elephant had reached her home. She saw Mr. Elephant surrounded by the herd. She knew they did it to keep her husband from a foolish rescue attempt.

She let out a soft trumpet call near his ear. Mr. Elephant's eyes popped open. He couldn't believe what he saw. He rubbed his eyes with his trunk just to be sure.

Mrs. Elephant stood in the circle of elephants. One-by-one all the elephants began to wake up. They were shocked. No elephant had ever escaped the humans.

"How did you rescue her?" the oldest elephant asked Mr. Elephant.

"It wasn't him," Mrs. Elephant answered, "although, I know he would give his life for me. Yet, he isn't big enough to defeat the guns of man. No elephant is big enough; nevertheless, one elephant is small enough. That elephant is my terrific, trunkless, toothy son!"

Across the valley lived the mouse family. Their only child was extremely large for his age. He also had a very long nose; nevertheless, his family was cheering too. Although he was too large to sneak by cats, he had just pulled off a daring rescue of his mother by slinging a slew of savage cats away with his greatly overgrown nose.

"No mouse was small enough to get by the cats, but my son was big enough to toss them out of the jungle!" claimed Mrs. Mouse.

"If only he could work for peanuts," sighed Mr. Mouse.

Fable:

The Elephant and Her Son

An elephant once gave birth to a mouse. "My child is too small to do anything an elephant should do," complained the elephant. All the other elephant mothers proudly showed off their children. In her shame, the mouse's mother kept her child hidden.

One day, some men came into the jungle. They captured the mother elephant and tied her up securely, planning to take her away. None of the elephants could save her because they feared the men. Yet, her child sneaked into the camp at night completely unnoticed.

He gnawed through every rope. As the last rope dropped off, the elephant fled into the jungle with her child tucked behind her ear. The mother was freed because her child was small enough to do something the elephants could not.

Life's small disappointments can bring big blessings.

Bobcat Cowboys Bad Hare Day

Story and illustrations by
Brian Davis

The Annual Carrot Harvest Festival is beginning in Rowdent Gulch. Most of the critters are busy getting ready for the big carrot chili cook-off. A couple of hare hair stylist are up to foul play with the Fowl Players. Meanwhile, the bobcat cowboys are cooking up their own batch of trouble.

Vocabulary Words

annual
calico
commotion
festival
governor
predator
prey
register
thespian
tuition

Chapter 1

Registration Forms

Otto Muskrat was wheeling and dealing with the customer on the other side of the counter.

"Okay, it looks like you filled out everything on the carpet order and registered for our free drawing," said Otto. "You'll steal the carpet from my store when it comes in this week."

"Right," said Bubba. "Just like the last time."

"I'll leave the door unlocked. Bobbybill messed it up last time I locked the door when you were planning on robbing me," explained Otto.

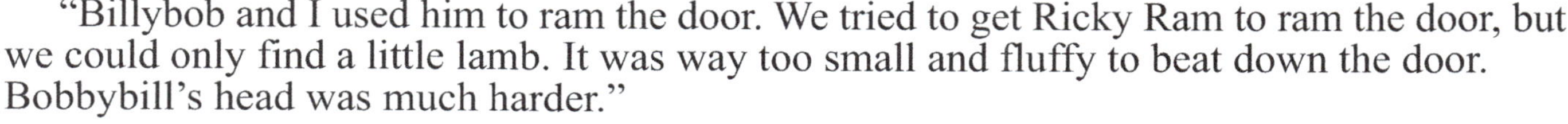

"Billybob and I used him to ram the door. We tried to get Ricky Ram to ram the door, but we could only find a little lamb. It was way too small and fluffy to beat down the door. Bobbybill's head was much harder."

"Ricky Ram was probably over at the diner mixing the pancake batter," guessed Otto Muskrat.

"That battering ram does make good pancakes," commented Davey Beaver who was listening as he worked in the store. "I like the ones where he uses sawdust instead of flour."

"We do have that big pancake breakfast coming up. I'll give the sheep a key in case I forget and lock the door," said Otto. "Now, if you're going to steal the carpet, I'm going to have to charge more for the padding and insulation."

Bubba nodded in agreement, "You've got to make a living. Just write up the total and leave the money in the cash register. Bobbybill will need to rob it to pay you."

Davey Beaver was sweeping the floor and listening. "Pardon me partner. I don't mean to impose, but that just doesn't make sense."

"Why not?" asked Otto and Bubba at the same time.

"The bobcats steal new carpet," Davey repeated. "Then, they steal the money from you to pay for padding and insulation."

"Yes, that sounds right," said Otto.

"It doesn't make a lick of sense," argued Davey. "Insulation is something you put in walls. Carpets are something you put on floors."

"You're right," said Otto. "Now, how am I going to make any profit off of this?"

"You could charge for installation," suggested Davey.

"That's brilliant! It's really hard to get insulation inside the solid rock walls of the bobcat's cave. It would have cost me a fortune," said Otto. "How did you get so smart all of the sudden?"

"I've been eating the old wooden schoolhouse," answered Davey Beaver. "There's a lot of learning in those walls."

"That's why I've noticed fewer chewed up broom handles around here," Otto observed.

"Why do you need new carpet anyway?" Davey asked Bubba Bobcat. "Didn't you just steal some last month?"

"I accidentally spilled spot remover on it," explained Bubba. "Without spots it just doesn't look very bobcat-like. At least I didn't spill it on Bobbybill this time. I spilled some on him when he was four. Momma made him live with the cougars until the spots came back. He just didn't look quite right for a month."

Otto checked his notes for the carpet order, "You're in luck, Bubba. I just had our drawing for the contest. You won free delivery on every theft over $20 this week. You and your brothers won't have to lug that heavy carpet all the way back to your cave on Gooseberry Mountain."

Bubba smiled, "That's mighty generous of you. It's that kind of service that keeps my brothers coming back to rob you!"

"You won the prize fair and square," said Otto. "But, maybe I should make my contests last more then ten minutes. It might give other customers a chance to enter."

While Bubba was at the store, his brothers Billybob and Bobbybill Bobcat were in another part of Rowdent Gulch. As Bubba left, he knew right where to find them. The bell in the town square was clanging loudly. Someone would clang the bell every time there was trouble in town. Bubba knew if there was trouble, Billybob and Bobbybill couldn't be too far away.

The trouble started as Billybob and Bobbybill tried to register for a booth at the Annual Carrot Harvest Festival. There must have been over a hundred rodents waiting in line. It took the bobcat brothers a couple of minutes to budge their way to the registration table in the town square. It was a lot of working tripping, pushing, and scaring the smaller animals out of the way. Deputy Guinea Pig and Walt Woodchuck sat at the table.

"We go to all the trouble of setting up a predator's registration table so you wouldn't cut in front of all the smaller critters," scowled Deputy Guinea Pig.

“You need to see Larry the Rat at the predator table,” Walt Woodchuck firmly stated. “This table is for registration of prey only.”

“Did Wilber Wolf come here to pray before eating?” asked Bobbybill. “He just pointed over at this table.”

“He couldn’t talk. His mouth was full,” explained Billybob.

“Except for that rat tail toothpick sticking out of his mouth,” added Bobbybill.

“Rat tail toothpick!” exclaimed Deputy Guinea Pig. “Clang the bell. I need Sheriff Prairie Dog at the predator registration table!”

Soon, Wilber Wolf had two double barrel rubber band slinging shotguns pointed right at him. The wolf reluctantly opened his mouth. The slobber covered rat plopped down on the registration table. The sheriff and deputy hauled the wolf off to jail.

“What did I do wrong?” cried the wolf.

“It’s illegal to eat registration table workers,” explained Deputy Guinea Pig. “It makes everyone in line have to wait too long while we hire a replacement. If we let you get away with it, the next thing you know critters will be eating guinea pig registration table workers. I just can’t let that happen.”

At that moment Babs Bluejay landed next to Larry the rat. She had missed all the commotion.

“I’m here to relieve you for lunch,” Babs explained to Larry.

“I’ve already been lunch,” quivered the rat. “I’m taking the rest of the day off,” he said as he ran toward his home.

Babs sighed heavily at the table. “How did wolf slobber get on these registration forms? That rat and his friends sure are messy.” She gathered the papers and without looking up yelled, “Next!”

Billybob and Bobbybill stepped up to the table.

Babs looked up and got a surprised look on her face. “Do you want a booth at the Carrot Harvest Festival? You do know that the critters can’t be forced to come to a booth.”

“It’s not for us,” Billybob explained.

“Although we did think of opening a kissin’ booth,” Bobbybill smiled.

"Until we found out the Hawg family was willing to be our customers," Billybob explained. "I hate gettin' my lips muddy."

"If it's for Bubba, I guess he'll do all right," said Babs. "Is he going to serve his pineapple, marshmallow burgers? Everybody loves those."

"That's the plan," said Billybob. "It's an honest way to make a livin', but he insists on doin' it."

"Sometimes I just don't understand that bobcat brother of mine," agreed Bobbybill. "Next thing you know he'll be depositing money in a bank instead of robbin' it."

"Just fill out the form and give me the registration fee," said Babs.

"We don't have the registration fee," explained Billybob. "We were going to rob you for it."

Babs sighed, "Then, I'm afraid you're in the wrong line. You'll have to get in the prey registration line. When you get to the front, just prey on the registration table workers. Rob them and bring the registration fee back to me."

"We just stood in that line," complained Bobbybill. "They sent us here."

"Did you explain to them that you needed to steal the money?" asked Babs.

Billybob stared down at the ground shamefully, "Well no, we just assumed they knew we were going to steal the money."

"We did tell them a wolf ate Larry the Rat," Bobbybill explained. "They came right over and rescued the rat."

"And they didn't make you stand in line at the 'Report a Registration Worker Eaten table?" asked Babs. "I'm going to have to go over our line waiting procedures with Walt and Guinea Pig. Next!"

At that, a fox stepped up to the registration table. Billybob and Bobbybill headed back to the end of the prey line to start cutting and budging their way to the front.

Chapter 2

Billybob Thinks

"What took you so long?" asked Bubba.

"We had to stand in six lines to register your booth," said Bobbybill. "The predator line, prey line, the predator line, the prey line again."

"Then, they made us stand in a line just to get a form to rob them," said Billybob. "They said it would make it easier to track us down."

"That's silly," said Bubba. "Everyone already knows where our secret hideout is."

"I'm not sure I know," said Bobbybill. "I got lost on my way back home yesterday."

Billybob explained, "After we got the form, of course we had to wait in the prey line to rob them. Then we had to take the money we stole to the predator table. Finally, we registered for your booth."

"Why did you want me to get a booth anyway?" asked Bubba. "Everyone will be eating carrot chili from the chili cookoff. Why would they want one of my marshmallow pineapple burgers?"

"If they're hungry enough, they'll pay a fortune for your marshmallow pineapple burgers," laughed Billybob.

Bobbybill started laughing, "they'll be plenty hungry."

Bubba started laughing too, "But, they won't be hungry at all after eating all that carrot chili. We won't make any money at all! You stood in all those lines for nothin'."

"Hush-up Bubba," said Billybob. "Leave all the thinkin' to us."

"Do I have to do part of the thinkin'?" said Bobbybill. "Thinkin' gives me a headache."

"I forgot," said Billybob. "I'll do all the thinkin'."

Billybob looked at Bubba. The bobcat was turning blue in the face.

"What's wrong Bubba? Breathe!"

Bubba took a deep breath. After panting for a few seconds he spoke, "If you're going to do all the thinkin', you shouldn't wait so long to tell me to breathe. I could have suffocated!"

"I don't mean all the thinkin'. Just the thinkin' about getting the critters hungry enough to buy marshmallow pineapple burgers," explained Billybob.

"Oh," answered Bubba. "Then you better tell Bobbybill. He's turnin' purple."

"Breathe, Bobbybill!" yelled Billybob.

"He might need mouth to mouth recess-a-tation," cried Bubba. "Put your lips on his!"

Billybob looked at Bobbybill and frowned, "I'm gonna miss you, Brother."

Suddenly Bobbybill took a deep breathe, "Ouch! Not thinkin' gives me a headache, too. What am I going to do?"

Bubba picked up a small rock. He scratched the word *breathe* onto it. "Here you go, Bobbybill. This rock can do the thinkin' for you."

"It does look like a smart rock," said Bobbybill.

"It looks even smarter than you," commented Billybob.

"Thanks," answered Bobbybill.

An hour later, the three bobcats crouched behind the brush at the side of the road. They watched a cargo wagon enter the narrow pass. It was pulled by a team of four sheep. A calico cat was driving. Billybob was ready to launch the next part of his plan.

"On the count of five, we all jump out and stop the wagon," Billybob instructed his brothers. "One, two, seven, nine… uh…what comes next?" Billybob stared at his paws and tried to count his fingers. They were hard to see through his thick fur.

"I think the wagon comes next," answered Bubba.

At that moment, the wagon rumbled by them. The bobcats choked on the dust kicked up by the wagon wheels.

"Five!" yelled Billybob.

The three bobcats leaped from behind the bushes. They raced after the wagon. The three bobcats leaped onto the back of the wagon. Billybob let out a screech in the calico cat's ear.

The frightened calico cat leaped from the wagon. The reins dangled helplessly on the ground. The wagon was out of control. They were heading right for a cliff.

Bubba went into action. He jumped from sheep to sheep until he reached the lead sheep. The bobcat grabbed the sheep by the tail. The sheep slowed to a stop.

Bubba continued wrestling with the sheep.

"Bubba, stop that," said Billybob. "You know it's illegal to wrestle sheep while we're hijacking a wagon."

"Oh, yeah," said Bubba. "I forgot. We don't want to do anything illegal while we're stealin' stuff."

"We don't want critters calling us low-down, good-for-nothin' bobcats again," said Bobbybill. "That hurts our feelin's"

"Baaaad Bobcat," bleated the sheep.

"I'm sorry, sheep," Bubba apologized, "but, you are a pretty good wrestler."

Billybob grabbed the reins and climbed onto the bench. "Hitch that sheep back up. We need to get out of here. That calico cat will probably get Sheriff Prairie Dog on our tails."

"I don't think he'd fit on our tails," said Bubba. "They're too short."

"I mean the sheriff's goin' to hunt us down and lock us up," explained Billybob. "Do I have to do all the thinkin'?"

"Yes," answered Bobbybill. "I don't want another headache."

The three bobcats drove the wagon away. Bubba still wasn't clear on the plan.

"How is stealin' a wagon going to make all the critters at the Carrot Festival want to buy my marshmallow pineapple burgers?" asked Bubba.

"It's the cargo in the wagon that's going to make your booth popular. Just leave the thinkin' to me. We'll stash it in our cave until after the festival."

"But the sheriff will take the cargo back after we hide it in our secret hideout," said Bubba. "Shouldn't we hide it somewhere else?"

"Oh, that's right," said Billybob. "Good thinkin'."

"I'm sorry," said Bubba. "I was supposed to let you do all the thinkin'."

"That's ok," said Billybob. "We'll just pretend I thought of it."

"You're so smart," said Bubba.

"Why don't we take it to the old mill?" suggested Bobbybill.

"Bobbybill, you're not supposed to think," Bubba scolded him.

"Uh…It was my rock's idea," said Bobbybill.

"Is it alright for the rock to think?" Bubba asked Billybob.

"As long as it keeps me from having to put my lips on Bobbybill's, that rock can do anything it wants," said Billybob Bobcat.

"I'm glad we have such a smart rock," said Bubba. "When the other critters say we're dumb as rocks, I'll take that as a compliment."

Soon, the bobcats reached the old mill. It was a red building with a large waterwheel sticking out of the side. It hadn't been used since the Possum Creek dried up last year. Weeds grew up along side the building.

The bobcats unloaded the boxes. The three bobcats carried the wooden crates into the mill. They stacked the boxes in a corner. Billybob covered them with empty flour sacks.

Chapter 3

The Fowl Players

"Are they gone yet?" whispered Harriet Hare."

The other hare crept to the edge of the loft. He cautiously peered over the edge. He couldn't see anything moving below. His big ears twisted this way and that. Harry Hare could pick up on any sound. The rumble of the wagon was growing fainter.

"They're gone," said Harry the Hare.

Harriet let out a sigh of relief. "What were those bobcats doing here anyway? I was afraid they were looking for lunch."

"I think they were stashing their loot," said Harry. "Hopefully it's a chest full of goldfish. We could be rich!"

The hare climbed down the ladder to the bottom floor. He followed the bobcat footprints to the corner of the room. Harriet joined him. The hares tugged on an empty flour sack. It was covering a crate. The hares found more crates under more sacks.

"What have we here?" said Harry greedily.

"Wait," warned Harriet. "If we steal from the bobcats, they might get angry."

Harry thought for a moment, "I've got it. We steal the bobcat's loot, but we don't tell them. That way, they won't know it was us."

Harriet smiled, "What are we waiting for?"

Harry searched for something to pry open the boxes. There weren't any tools in the old mill. Harry remembered the tree outside the mill. He hopped outside.

At the base of the tree the hare let out a whistle. A black feathered head peeked over a nest.

"I need to open some wooden crates," Harry explained.

"Stand back," said the crow as it tossed a metal object out of the nest. It landed with a loud thud.

"Thanks for the crowbar," said Harry. "I'll bring it back shortly."

The hares hopped on the bar until the first lid popped off.

"Is it goldfish?" asked Harriet.

Harry dipped his paw into the box.

"It's just birdseed," he sighed.

"Maybe the next box," said Harriet hopefully.

Harry tried the next box. "It's not birdseed," he said in a disappointed voice. "It's cowboy hats."

Harriet tried one on. It covered her face. She pulled it off and read the tag. "It's a genuine ten gallon hat."

The hares opened box after box. Most of them were filled with more ten gallon hats. Some were filled with birdseed. The hares slumped against the boxes. They were tired from all the hopping on the crowbar.

"All that work for a bunch of useless hats and birdseed," sighed Harriet.

Just then, Harry's ears perked up. "Listen."

Harriet held her breath. Her ears twitched toward they road. "Oh, no! They're coming back. Quick, cover the boxes!"

Harry and Harriet tossed the flour sacks back over the boxes. Harry peered around the door. Sure enough, a wagon was heading right for the old mill. He stepped into the doorway.

"What are you doing? They'll see you," cried Harriet.

"It's a different wagon," said Harry. "A duck is driving it."

Harriet joined her husband at the door. She stared at the strange looking wagon. It looked like a small house on wheels. It was brightly painted. The wagon rolled to a stop. The duck hopped off his bench.

"Good day," he quacked as he hopped off the wagon.

The duck waddle to the back of the wagon and opened a door. He extended his wing and helped a goose out. She was followed by a chicken.

"Let us introduce ourselves," said the duck. "I am Mallard LaQuack. These are my fellow thespians, Golda Goose and Meg Egging."

"I am Harry Hare and this is my lovely wife, Harriet," the hare replied in a friendly tone.

Harriet stepped forward, "Pardon me, but what is a thespian? Is it some kind of bird?"

Mallard smiled, "No, my dear. A thespian is another name for actor. And I must say, I work with two of the loveliest and talented thespians around."

The other two birds blushed.

"What can we do for you?" asked Harriet. She was so excited to be in the presence of such greatness.

"Look at those eyes," said Mallard as he stared at Harriet.

"Mr. Hare has quite a look about him, too. Have the two of you ever done any acting?" asked Golda Goose.

"They seem like naturals," agreed Meg Egging, the chicken.

"Us, act?" said Harriet. "We don't know the first thing about acting."

"We can remedy that," said Mallard LaQuack. "That is precisely why we are here. Having achieved greatness on the stage, it is now our turn to give back."

"I don't understand," said Harry.

"What's not to understand?" said Golda. "We're offering you the opportunity to learn from greatness. We can teach anyone to act."

"I don't think I could ever act," said Harriet shyly.

"That's what everyone once thought of the Bobcat Cowboys. Yet, we taught them to act," said Mallard.

"We taught them to act like bears," said Meg. "Perhaps you caught them in their performance of Goldie Locks and the Three Bears."

"They played at the Rowdent Gulch Theatre for three weeks," Golda added. "They were magnificent after our instruction and inspiration."

"And you do all of this for free?" Harry asked suspiciously.

"Oh, No, my dear rabbit," said Mallard.

"Hare," correct Harriet. "It's a common mistake."

"There is a slight tuition fee," said Golda. "But true greatness comes at a price."

Harriet watched her husband. She knew the look on his face. He looked very doubtful. That disappointed her. Learning to be a thespian sounded like fun. It would be so much more fun than hiding out in the old mill all day.

Harry studied the wagon. In painted big letters were the words, The Fowl Players. It was coming back to him. The birds had run into some problems in Rowdent Gulch in the past. They had gotten mixed up with the Bobcat Cowboys. The birds had stolen some gold painted sleds from them.

The hare was very clever. He quickly formulated a plan. "We would be very interested in taking acting lessons."

Harriet was very surprised, "Really! That would be wonderful."

"That is wonderful," said Mallard. "Now about the tuition. We will need a bag of birdseed from both of you."

"I want to do more than just take lessons," said Harry. "I would like you to open an acting school right here in our mill. I have plenty of birdseed to invest."

The birds gasped with joy.

Mallard was almost breathless, "You are a dream come true. A bunny with money!"

"What play should we start with?" Golda asked Meg.

"We want to learn to act like a hair stylist," Harry announced. "Can you do that?"

The birds looked puzzled.

"I have three cases of birdseed," said Harry.

"We can teach you to be a most convincing hair stylist," said Meg.

"Although we don't know how to actually cut hair. Feathers we can style, but fur?" Golda cautioned them.

"That's alright," said Harry. "Let's unload your wagon and get started."

The birds and hares unloaded the wagon into the mill. Soon, the hares were learning to act like hairdressers.

Chapter 4

Ten Gallon Hats

Early in the morning, Billybob and Bobbybill crept up to the old mill. They saw the wagon and were afraid Sheriff Prairie Dog had come to take the loot. They watched as Harriet and Harry loaded the crates.

"Not today," moaned Billybob. "They'll have the ten gallon vats in time for the Carrot Chili Cookoff."

"If the critters fill up on chili, when will they be hungry for Bubba's marshmallow pineapple burgers?"

"There's only one thing to do," said Billybob.

"Eat carrot chili?" asked Bobbybill.

"No," said Billybob. "We've got to steal that funny looking wagon. We can't let those hares take it back to town."

The bobcats snuck up to the wagon. Harry had just closed the door in back. Harriet was already inside the boxed-in wagon. They wanted to sneak away before the birds woke up. As Harry walked to the front, the bobcats leaped onto the driver's bench. They grabbed the reins, and the wagon took off.

"Oh no!" cried Harry. "My dear Harriet has been bunny-knapped."

He took off after the wagon. His swift feet allowed him to catch up quickly. He hopped onto the back of the wagon. Harry climbed to the roof. He crept to the front of the wagon and peered over the edge. The hare let out a gasp.

He ducked back and took a minute to think. The hare was smart and quickly formulated a plan. He swung his big back feet over the edge of the roof. The hare leaned forward and pushed off.

Harry plopped right in between Billybob and Bobbybill. The surprised bobcats pulled back on the reins. The wagon came to a halt.

"What are you doing here?" Billybob asked.

"I'm doing you a big favor," said Harry.

"I saw you loading up our loot. You were going to take it back to Sheriff Prairie Dog. We stole it fair and square," said Billybob.

"I'm sorry to hear you admit that you stole all those hats," said Harry.

"Hats?" said Billybob nervously. "We didn't steal hats. We stole ten gallon vats."

"That's right," said Bobbybill. "We were in the store when Otto Muskrat took down the order for them. Deputy Guinea Pig ordered them for the Carrot Chili Cookoff."

"Otto even spelled it out to be sure," said Billybob. "He spelled vats, h-a-t-s, vats."

Harry just frowned.

"Oh no!" cried Bobbybill as he pulled out his thinkin' rock. "My rock says h-a-t-s spells hats, not vats. Otto ordered the wrong thing, again."

Billybob and Bobbybill began to shake.

Harry looked at them, "I see you are aware of the governor's new anti-hat stealing law."

"Yes," whimpered Billybob and Bobbybill.

The new law had just passed. Hat stealin' was now punishable by de-furring. A bear who stole a picnic basket that contained a hat was the first to be de-furred. The bobcats remembered laughing at the picture of the bare bear in the newspaper. It didn't seem so funny now.

"It just so happens, my wife and I are hare stylists. We can each shave one of you. Let's get it over quickly."

"Please don't do it. Winter is comin' soon. We're going to need our fur," begged Billybob. "We promise we'll never do anything bad ever again."

"Or at least for the next few hours," added Bobbybill.

The hare rubbed his chin. He appeared to be thinking it over. The bobcats tried to look as sweet and innocent as possible. They batted their eyes and put their paws together to beg.

Harry sighed, "I guess I can get the governor to pardon you. But, I will need to take the hats."

The bobcats smiled, "Thank you!"

"Now move along," said Harry. "And remember, you promised to be good for several hours."

Harry took the reins from the bobcats. They scurried off into the brush. Harry yelled giddy-up. The wagon took off for Rowdent Gulch.

"Why did you say we would be good for hours?" said Billybob Bobcat to Bobbybill. "How are we expected to do that?"

"But, you said we'd never do anything bad again. That's a lot longer than a few hours," Bobbybill argued.

"But, I was lyin'," said Billybob. "See what happens when I don't do all the thinkin'. We have to be good for hours. How are we going to do that?"

"I don't know," said Bobbybill. "Should we ask my rock?"

The wagon rolled into town the day of the Carrot Festival. After visiting the registration table, Harry was ready to open his shop. He set up a tent in back of the wagon.

Harry and Harriet hung a banner. It read: Harry and Harriet Hare's Mobile Hair Salon Best Hairdo Contest. First Place, 1,000 Goldfish. Free hair styling for Carrot Chili Cookoff Contestants.

Starlet Fussybunny O'Hare and her sister Scarlet Fussybunny were the first to see the sign. They could never resist a free hair styling. They were tired from carrying their buckets of carrots anyway. They decided they should feel extra pretty for the Carrot Chili Cookoff. Plus, they would love to go on a shopping spree with 1,000 goldfish to spend.

The sisters were led into the tent by Harriet Hare. Harriet and Harry had them sit in chairs with their backs to each other. "You mustn't peek at each other's hair style until the judging in the contest," explained Harry.

"Just do a good job, or my husband will sue you," giggled Starlet.

"He's the famous lawyer, Frazzle O'Hare," Scarlet added.

"Just trust us," said Harry. "It's not like this is the first time we've every styled hair."

"But, it is the first time," corrected Harriet.

Starlett and Scarlet looked a little nervous. They were real fussy bunnies about their hair. They started to get up.

Harry placed his paws on their shoulders and pushed them back down into the chair. "What she means is every styling is like the first time for us. It's like a new adventure.

We have fresh, bold ideas. You deserve an original and special hair styling. Loveliness like yours needs to be expressed in something artistic, not ordinary."

Harry was really starting to see the acting lessons pay off. He was very believable. The sisters were getting excited again. The two hares relaxed as Harry and Harriet went to work.

The Hares snipped with scissors above the sister's heads. They combed through the fur. Finally, Harry and Harriet sprayed Starlet and Scarlet's hair.

"That should just about do it," said Harry.

"Let us see," said Starlet and Scarlet.

"The contest rules state that no one can see the hair styles before the judging," Harry explained.

"And besides," Harriet added. "The hair spray will make your hair fall out if it is exposed to light before it dries."

"How long does it take to dry?" asked Scarlet.

"Just a few hours," said Harry.

"We can't stay here for a few hours," explained Starlet. "We're in the carrot chili cookoff."

"That is a problem," sighed Harry. "What can we do about it? What can we do about it…" he glanced and nodded at Harriet.

Mrs. Hare suddenly remembered her part, "I know. You can cover it with a hat."

"We don't have hats with us," said Scarlet.

"I get it," said Starlet angrily. "You give a free hairstyling, and then sell us hats. I knew there was a catch. I will have my dear Frazzle sue you!"

"We would never do such a thing," said Harry. Although, it sounded like a good idea to him. "We will gladly give you a hat."

Chapter 5

Hare Hair-dos

Harriet hopped out the back of the tent. She went into the wagon and grabbed two of the ten gallon hats.

"Harriet is a specialist at putting on hats. She'll arrange them on you so you'll look lovely until the hair spray dries," Harry promised. "I will tidy up the tent a bit while she finishes."

Harriet plopped a hat on the heads of Starlet and Scarlet. The large, ten gallon hats landed on their shoulders. Meanwhile, Harry grabbed the buckets of carrots the sisters had brought to the carrot chili cookoff.

He carried them into the wagon. Harry dumped the carrots into a crate and filled the buckets up with rocks. The hare entered the tent again.

"I can't see anything with this huge hat on," said Scarlet.

"Neither can I," said Starlet.

"Perfect," said Harry. "That way you'll know that no light is shining on your hair. You can also watch it dry."

"Oh, that makes sense," said Starlet.

Harry handed them their buckets full of rocks. The sisters spread the news about the free hair styles, best hairdo contest, and even the free hats. Soon there was a line waiting outside the tent.

All the critters wanted a free hairstyling. Harry and Harriet acted like they were giving the animals hair styles. The animals would walk in with buckets of carrots. They walked out with buckets of rocks. They never noticed because none of them could see.

The hares worked all afternoon. They eventually ran out of rocks. Mrs. Mink was the last customer. Harry had to fill her bucket with firewood. In the process, the wagon was filling up with all the carrots in Rowdent Gulch. Harry's plan was working perfectly.

Billybob and Bobbybill crouched atop a building in town. They watched Harry Hare make several trips from the tent to the wagon. Each time he carried a bucket.

"What do you think is in the buckets?" asked Bobbybill.

"Well," said Billybob, "The hares are giving hair cuts. I would say the buckets are full of fur. Has it been a few hours yet?"

"I hope so," said Bobbybill. "I don't think I can stay out of trouble much longer."

"Good," said Billybob. "Because we're going to steal that wagon."

"Why do we want a wagon full of fur?" asked Bobbybill.

"In case the governor doesn't give us a pardon after all. I want to have plenty of extra fur if we get de-furred for hat stealin'," Billybob explained.

Harry and Harriet packed up the tent. They were hurrying to get out of town. Just as they were finishing, Sheriff Prairie Dog came up.

"Thank you so much for all the free hair styling," said Sheriff Prairie Dog. "The whole town is excited to find out who wins the 1,000 goldfish. Come on up to the grandstand and sit with me. You can judge the winner right after the Carrot Chili Contest."

Harry and Harriet squirmed. They wanted to get out of town before the hats came off.

"It's been an interesting Carrot Festival," said the sheriff as he walked them to the grandstand. "The critters have been bumping into things all day long. But it was awfully nice of you to give them all hats."

Walt Woodchuck, Davey Beaver, and Otto Muskrat were judging the Carrot Chili Contest. They began with the Fussybunny's chili pot. The three judges each took a bite. They immediately spit it out.

"That tastes like rocks!" said Walt.

"Why I never!" said a voice from under a hat. "Who said that? It's a good thing I can't see you."

The judges moved from pot to pot. Each time it was the same thing. They all tasted like rocks. Finally, they reached Mrs. Minks Carrot Chili Pot.

Walt took a sip, "We'll it doesn't taste like rocks."

Otto took a sip, "It doesn't taste like carrot chili either."

Davey Beaver took a sip. He got a chip of firewood in his spoon. "Mmm…hickory. I think this one tastes the best."

"Well, it does taste the least worst," said Otto. "It has my vote."

Walt agreed, "Mrs. Mink is the winner. Where are you Mrs. Mink?"

A ten gallon hat started jumping up and down.

Deputy Guinea Pig guided her to the grandstand to pick up her trophy.

"I want to thank all those who made this possible," said Mrs. Mink from beneath the hat. "Thank you Bubba Bobcat for donating the pots to cook the chili in."

All the critters cheered. Bubba was glad to help out when he found out the vats were missing.

Mrs. Mink continued, "Thank you Otto Muskrat for ordering the Bobcats Cowboys carpet with pots instead of carpet with spots." She paused as the crowd cheered again. "And thank you Harry and Harriet Hare for the hairdos and hats."

The crowd cheered even louder. Sheriff Prairie Dog smiled and put his arm on Harry's shoulder. The hare just wanted to get away.

"Is it safe to take off the hats now?" asked the sheriff.

Harry reluctantly nodded yes. The critters pulled off the hats. The hares had actually only used water to spray the fur. Wet fur under hats all day made some very strange looking hat hair hairdos on the critters. Harry thought they all looked silly.

The other critters didn't think so. Everyone liked their own hair style the best. It was a good thing the sheriff had placed some mirrors on the grandstand.

"Harry and Harriet will now announce the winner of the 1,000 goldfish prize," said Sheriff Prairie Dog.

Harry never planned on being in town long enough to announce a winner. He also didn't have 1000 goldfish. All he had was a wagon full of carrots. He wished he was on it heading back to the mill. The hare studied the crowd. He saw Starlet O'Hare standing next to her husband, Frazzle.

The hare was afraid if he didn't pick her he would be sued. He also knew he may need a good lawyer very soon. He whispered in Harriet's ear. She nodded in agreement.

"We pick Starlet Fussybunny O'Hare," announced Harry.

Starlet jumped up and down. Scarlet gave her a big hug.

Harry turned to the sheriff. "We left the goldfish in our wagon. We'll go get them and be right back."

Harry and Harriet hopped off the grandstand. They cut through the crowd. Deputy Guinea Pig followed them. He wanted to provide security for the goldfish. He hadn't seen Billybob and Bobbybill all afternoon. He thought they might be up to something.

The hares reached the place where they had left the wagon. It was gone. Deputy Guinea Pig caught up with them. Starlet and Frazzle followed, too.

"Oh, no!" cried Starlet, "We've been robbed."

Chapter 6

String'em Up

The wagon that looked like a little house on wheels pulled up in front of the cave. Mallard, Golda, and Meg sat on a tree limb and watched. Billybob and Bobbybill were driving it.

"I knew those bobcats stole our wagon from the mill," quacked Mallard.

"We should have gotten as far away as possible from Rowdent Gulch when we had a chance," clucked Meg.

"We just finished serving our time in the concession stand and now we have to deal with those bobcats again," honked Golda Goose.

"We couldn't travel too far," Mallard argued. "We had no money and no food. It's a good thing we met the Hares. At least we've been well fed."

"And it was fun to teach Harry and Harriet to act," cackled Meg.

As soon as the bobcats went inside the cave, the birds swooped out of the tree. They landed on the bench on the front of the wagon. Mallard grabbed the reins and quickly turned the wagon around.

Sheriff Prairie Dog had formed a posse. A whole group of critters were heading up Gooseberry Mountain. They were sure the Bobcat Cowboys were behind the wagon theft. A few yards from the cave, the posse met the wagon. Mallard LaQuack stopped. He flew off the bench and landed by Sheriff Prairie Dog.

"The bobcats stole our wagon," Mallard tried to explain.

Deputy Guinea Pig opened the back door. He was greeted by a tidal wave of carrots. The deputy was up to his ears in carrots.

"I think I found something," he mumbled from under the pile.

The sheriff looked at the birds. "It seems like you've been caught red winged. I think you need to have another talk with the judge."

Billybob and Bobbybill heard the commotion and came out of the cave.

"What's going on?" asked Billybob.

"I have to apologize this time," said the sheriff. "We thought you stole a wagon load of carrots. I formed this posse here to come take you in. It turns out the Fowl Players stole the carrots. They filled up their wagon with them."

"We would never steal a wagon load of carrots," said Billybob.

"We stole a wagon load of fur," Bobbybill explained.

"String'em up anyway," came a voice from the posse.

"Is that you, Bubba?" asked Billybob.

"Hi Billybob," said Bubba. "Everyone was talking about stringin' you up. I like string. You can use it to tie shoes, if we wore shoes. You can put strings on banjos and guitars. We could put dried macaroni on it and make necklaces. I was hopin' they'd give us a whole bunch of strings."

"Mother's day is coming up," said Bobbybill. "Momma would like a new macaroni necklace."

By now the critters were getting hungry. It was too late to cook carrot chili. The rock soup wasn't very tasty. Davey Beaver ate all the hickory stew that Mrs. Mink made.

Sheriff Prairie Dog had an idea. He had all the critters go home and get a piece of string. They all gathered around Bubba's booth back at the Carrot Festival. The bobcat cooked up lots of marshmallow pineapple burgers. The cost of the burgers was a piece of string. Peppy Possum very thoughtfully brought some macaroni from Peppy's Pizza and Pasta Parlor. Bessybob Bobcat was going to love her new necklace.

Billybob and Bobbybill spread out their new spotless carpet. They invited all the critters to eat on it. Bubba topped all the burgers with brown mushroom gravy. The drippings made for lots of spots. The bobcats watched as their carpet became spotted to perfection.

Judge Polecat and Frazzle O'Hare were busy the next week. The Hares were on trial for distributing hats without a permit. Frazzle successfully defended them. He pointed out the law actually said you can't distribute vats without a permit. Although the law was meant to stop illegal hat distribution, Otto Muskrat's brother had typed the law.

Next, Starlet hired her husband, Frazzle to sue the Hares for her 1000 goldfish prize for the best hairdo. Harry and Harriet couldn't pay of course. Judge Polecat ordered the Hares to earn the money by styling hair. Frazzle was happy to win two cases in a week.

Frazzle's best customers came next. Billybob, Bobbybill, and Bubba were on trail for scaring a calico cat on a Thursday. The calico cat's terrifying account was winning over the jury. Frazzle entered a plea agreement for the bobcats. They agreed to sweep up the fur in the Hare's styling salon for the next two months. Billybob and Bobbybill were very pleased with the decision. They got to keep the fur. It was great insurance against a de-furring.

The last trial featured the Fowl Players. They were on trial for carrot-knapping. Frazzle once again prevailed, but only because of a technicality. None of the carrots would testify against them. So once again, the Fowl Players packed up their little house on wheels.

The wagon started down the street. Suddenly, a critter with a ten gallon hat pulled over its eyes stepped right in front of the wagon. Mallard stopped abruptly, too abruptly. Judge Polecat had just bought one of those new-fangled sheepless carriages. When the wagon stopped, the carriage crashed right into the back of it.

The air filled the pungent odor of angry skunk. The Fowl Players knew there was no point in even arguing. The birds hopped off the wagon, put on their aprons, and headed back to the theatre. It was time to get the concession stand ready for the next show. All in all it was just another typical day in Rowdent Gulch.

Story and illustrations by
Brian Davis

A young girl and her mother move to a mysterious house to take care of a sick aunt. While exploring the rooms in the house, Hannah discovers a secret. It leads her on a journey that will take courage, loyalty and an imaginary dog to complete.

Vocabulary Words

appreciation
bedposts
decorative
disorganized
emanate
fascinating
horizon
locksmith
nautilus
pantry
pondered
precarious
predicament
spiral
substitute
trampoline
tropical
Victorian
vegetation

Chapter 1

Accept No Substitutes

Hannah knew it was going to be one of those days at school from the first moment she walked into the classroom. First, it was noisier than normal. Then she noticed the stranger standing at the teacher's desk.

A few of the boys in her class loved to challenge substitutes. To Hannah, it seemed her teacher must pack their brains in her briefcase each night and take them home with her. The boys sure didn't seem to use them whenever she wasn't there. They never seemed to remember how much trouble they would be in when the teacher got back.

By the history lesson, the substitute was already pretty frazzled. Somehow the gerbil ended up in her lunch sack. Then, the lesson plan book got mysteriously placed on the bookshelf.

The teacher wasn't able to teach the history lesson. In fact, she didn't even know there was a history lesson. That suited Hannah just fine. It was her least favorite subject. She thought it was so boring to learn about things that had already happened. It was too late to change any of it so what was the use?

Finally, someone flipped all the schedules around. The substitute took the students to the music room for P.E. She took the class to the library at music time. No one spoke up to correct her until the class reached the different parts of the building.

Things started to settle down after lunch. As always, Hannah was the first one finished with her spelling assignment. She raised her hand and asked if she could get a book from the reading center. Hannah walked to the back corner of the room. A rustling sound came from the closet.

Hannah peeked around the corner. Somehow James and Braydon had slipped into the coat closet without being noticed by the substitute. They were pulling Hoppity, the black and white rabbit, out of its cage. Braydon looked up and saw Hannah.

He put his finger to his mouth to signal for her to be quiet. James looked up, too. He waved a fist at Hannah. It was a warning not to talk. Hannah picked up the first book she could find and rushed back to her desk.

Although she kept her nose buried in the book, she did notice James and Braydon sneak back to their seats. Hannah worried about Hoppity. He was such a lovable rabbit. Surely, the boys wouldn't have hurt the rabbit. Then again, they were pretty mean.

Most of the class referred to them as "double trouble". She tried to stay clear of them as much as possible. A few of the girls hung around with them. Hannah could see why. They were just about as mean as the boys. They often called her names and made fun of her clothes.

Hannah's father was in another country. He was in the army. That wasn't his main job. He was in the reserves, but his unit was sent to protect people thousands of miles away. Sometimes Hannah wished he were home so he could protect her.

Since the army didn't pay as much as her father's regular job, her mom had to save money. One way they did this was by buying used clothes. They were nice enough, they just weren't the newest. Some of her dresses were a little faded and worn. Hannah understood that she was growing quickly. Her clothes would be replaced soon enough.

"Everyone put away your spelling books. Clear your desks. It's time for recess," instructed the substitute teacher.

She called one row of students at a time to get their jackets from the coat closet. When Hannah's row was called, James cut in line ahead of her. Braydon was in back of her. Hannah had an uneasy, queasy feeling in her stomach. As soon as they were out of sight of the teacher, James turned around.

"You saw nothing, and if you say anything…" James waved his fist at her.

The students waited in line at the door. The teacher walked back to the closet. She came back out holding her coat. The substitute slipped it on and reached into her pocket for her gloves.

Suddenly, she started screaming and dancing around. The teacher was trying to get the coat off as quickly as possible. It landed on the floor. All the students jumped back.

"There's something alive in the pocket!" one of the students shouted when she saw it move.

A few of the students jumped on top of their desks. The teacher got her pointer stick and prodded at her coat. That was when Hoppity decided to make his escape. He ran full speed around the classroom and right out the door. The students chased after their class pet into the hallway.

Mr. Kraig stepped from the principal's office to see what the commotion was all about. He was nearly knocked flat by the running students. Then the substitute walked up to him and pointed her finger in his face.

"This is the worst class I have ever substituted in. I don't ever want to come back. They're all yours for the rest of the day!"

The principal rounded up the students and ushered them back to the classroom. One of the boys put Hoppity back in its cage. Hannah had never seen the principal look this angry. He walked slowly up and down the aisles. His arms were crossed, and he sighed deeply.

"Does someone want to tell me how a rabbit ended up in Ms. Anderson's coat pocket?" The principal looked slowly over the class. He peered into the eyes of every student.

Hannah slowly raised her hand.

"Yes?"

She was about to speak when James kicked her chair leg. Braydon made a fist and squeezed it tightly. Hannah began to shake.

"Is Hoppity alright?"

"The rabbit is fine, but he could have gotten injured," frowned the principal. "I'm very upset with this class. Ms. Anderson is a good substitute teacher. She has never had a problem like this before. This class should be ashamed of itself."

"Now, someone needs to explain what happened with the rabbit. Don't make me punish the whole class."

No one raised their hand. Only three people knew what happened. The boys didn't want to get punished. Hannah didn't want the boys to punish her.

The principal waited a few minutes. "If that's the way you want it. Everyone take out a piece of paper. You will write an apology letter to Ms. Anderson."

One of the girls raised her hand, "Is that our punishment?"

"Oh no," said Mr. Kraig, "I'll be talking to your teacher when she gets back. This is only the beginning of your punishment. I want to put some thought into what should happen with this class."

Chapter 2

Out on a High Note

Hannah was surprised when she got home. Her apartment was empty. There were just a few suitcases by the front door.

"Mom?" Hannah called out.

There was no answer. She went room to room. Everything was empty. Hannah started to panic.

"Mom!" she cried.

Suddenly, she heard a key in the lock of the door. Hannah was even more afraid. The doorknob turned. Hannah ran to the bathroom and locked the door.

She heard footsteps. They grew closer. Hannah cowered in the bathtub. Somebody tried to turn the doorknob. Hannah heard a scratching sound inside the lock.

The lock could be opened with a small screwdriver. Hannah's mom had to do it once when the door was accidentally closed when no one was inside. It just took a little twist. Hannah started to cry.

The door burst open. The shower curtain was suddenly pulled back. Hannah's arms were covering her face.

"Hannah! Are you all right?"

Hannah opened her eyes. Her mother was staring at her with a very concerned look.

"Mom! It's you. I was so scared."

"Honey, I told you I might be a couple of minutes late today," her mother reminded her.

"But where is everything?" Hannah sobbed. "I thought you were kidnapped, along with all our furniture."

"Our plans have changed," her mother explained.

"Is Dad, okay?"

"What would make you ask that?" said her mom.

"I worry about him," said Hannah.

"He's fine," said her mom. "But Aunt Millie had a little spell. So, I decided we would go a few weeks early. I was able to get the movers to come in today. All our things are in storage."

“I’m not going back to school?” asked Hannah.

“No, I’m sorry you didn’t get to say goodbye,” her mom said sympathetically.

Hannah smiled. “Do you think the principal is still in his office?”

“School hasn’t been out very long. I imagine Mr. Kraig would still be there. Why do you ask?”

“Can I call him?” asked Hannah.

“I didn’t realize you were that close to him. Do you want to tell him goodbye?”

“I want to give him a little present,” smiled Hannah.

“We won’t have time to stop by,” said Hannah’s mom.

“I can give him the present over the phone,” said Hannah.

Her mom pulled out her cell phone and punched in the number. She had a puzzled look on her face as she handed Hannah the phone.

“Are you sure I won’t be going back to school?” Hannah asked one more time.

Her mom nodded.

“Mr. Kraig,” Hannah spoke into the phone. “Braydon and James did it. I would have told you in class, but they threatened to punch me. They also put the hamster in Ms. Anderson’s lunch sack.”

“Thank you,” said Mr. Kraig. “You’ve saved all the other classmates a lot of punishment. It sounds like I need to make a couple of phone calls.”

Hannah was smiling when she hung up the phone.

“I don’t know what that was about,” said Hannah’s mom. “But that’s the first time I’ve seen you smile about moving.”

Hannah had been upset about moving. She didn’t want to go to a strange place and have to make new friends. Her father had never been to Aunt Millie’s house. What if he didn’t know where to find them? What if someone stole all their stuff while it was in storage?

There was so much to be afraid of; she didn’t know where to start. Aunt Millie was her mom’s aunt. Hannah had never met her. What if she didn’t like little girls? Hannah had been worrying for weeks.

Still, being able to finally tell on James and Braydon made it all worthwhile. She could just imagine them in the principal’s office. For once, they would be the ones who were afraid. They would never be able to get even with her. She would be seen as a hero in the eyes of her classmates. It was beautiful.

Hannah and her mom were on the road that afternoon. They had no furniture, so they had nowhere to sleep in their apartment. Her mom figured if they had to sleep in a hotel, they might as well get a little closer to Aunt Millie’s.

Putting more distance between her and James and Braydon was fine with Hannah. She never knew where she might run into them. Hannah was making her great escape. Twenty-four hours of driving should be a safe enough distance. By late tomorrow evening, she should be completely safe.

She wondered what Aunt Millie would be like. All she knew about her was that Aunt Millie had been sick. Hannah's mom was a nurse, so she was going to take care of her. Hannah's mom hadn't seen her aunt in several years because they lived so far away. All Hannah knew was that her mom's aunt lived in a big house. Aunt Millie had plenty of money and could easily afford to pay Hannah's mom more than she had been making. Plus, they could live with her.

Hannah's mom drove late into the night. They stayed at a hotel near the highway. After an early morning breakfast, they were back on the road. Hannah and her mom had good talks on the road. Hannah told all about the bunny episode. Her mom laughed when Hannah explained the phone call.

"I guess you can say you went out on a high note," said her mom.

"What does that mean?" asked Hannah.

"It means you were at your best at the very end."

Hannah's mom was glad Hannah told the principal; nevertheless, she gave her some advice for the future.

"Don't ever be afraid to do the right thing," her mother explained. "You'll meet lots of people like James and Braydon in your lifetime. They get away with things because of fear. You've got to have courage."

"I'm too afraid to have courage," Hannah explained. "I'm not like you and Dad."

"Hannah," her mother explained. "You can be afraid and have courage."

"I thought courage was not being afraid," said Hannah.

"Courage is doing what's right and good even though you're afraid. Did it take courage to eat breakfast this morning?" her mother asked.

"No, that's silly," said Hannah.

"Right," said her mother. "It only takes courage to do things you're afraid of."

"Like moving?" asked Hannah.

"No," said Hannah's mom. "That just takes a mom and a car."

Chapter 3

The New and Old Surroundings

Hannah watched the rain pour on the window sill. If she had been home, at least she could watch television or play with her toys. Hannah looked around the room. It was full of old things, antiques. They must have been valuable because her mom told her not to touch them.

They had arrived late the night before. It was the first time Hannah had ever seen the house in the daytime. Her mom described the house as Victorian. Hannah described it as scary looking. It was a large, old house that looked run down. It was just the type of house that people thought was haunted. The house looked like something out of a scary movie.

With nothing else to do, Hannah decided to explore her surroundings. She found her mother in her great aunt Millie's bedroom. Hannah's mother looked up from a book and put a finger to her lips to remind Hannah to be quiet. Four tall, dark bedposts framed the bed. A small, wrinkled woman lay asleep covered by a colorful old quilt. Aunt Millie needed her sleep.

Hannah moved on down the hall. She peered into the kitchen. It was a large room, bigger than most kitchens. The stove and refrigerator looked older than any she had ever seen. They looked like little cabinets on legs. The refrigerator had a large basket-like thing on top that was making a humming sound. The stove was made of iron and had lots of doors. It was like being in a museum for kitchen appliances.

"Maybe it's a good time to explore the snack supply," said Hannah to herself.

She began to open cabinet doors. Inside she found colorful dishes and bowls. Hannah thought they looked pretty, but definitely not very filling. She needed food, preferable junk food – chips, cookies, soda.

After a futile search of the cabinets, Hannah noticed a narrow door in the kitchen. It opened up into a pantry. The closet was lined with shelves full of glass jars. She could tell by all the colors that they held a variety of different foods. There were jellies, fruits, vegetables, and even some nuts. Each jar had a neatly printed label identifying the contents.

Aunt Millie must have canned all the food herself. Hannah admired the neat handwriting. Some even had decorative drawings on the labels. Hannah could tell they were hand drawn. She concluded that Aunt Millie was a very good artist.

In one corner of the closet were some boxes. Crackers, cereal, oatmeal, baking soda, salt and other basic boxed items were on the shelf. One box seemed quite out of place. Hannah picked up the colorful box and carefully opened it. Inside was a metal object. It was a toy sailboat.

She began to replace it on the shelf when she noticed something very odd. It was a small door, about the size of the boat's box. She reached out to touch it. That's when Hannah realized it wasn't a door at all. It was a painting of a door. She thought it to be a very odd place for a painting.

"You must be hungry."

The voice startled Hannah. She turned to see her mother standing in the pantry doorway. Hannah stuffed the box back onto the shelf. In the process, something began to roll. It landed at her feet and bounced back up to her knees. The red and yellow rubber ball came to rest at her feet.

She picked it up and looked sheepishly at her mother. For the first time, it struck Hannah that all the nosing around may have been very impolite. She didn't know Aunt Millie at all. Maybe young girls were not welcome to explore anywhere they chose.

"You go keep Aunt Millie company while I fix us all some lunch," said Hannah's mother. "She's awake now and very anxious to meet you. And guess what?"

"What?" asked Hannah.

"That's not a very good guess," her mom smiled. "Aunt Millie had the grocery store send over a fresh pineapple!"

Hannah loved fresh pineapples. She didn't get them very often. Her mom also made the best pineapple upside down cake. So, they always saved some slices back for a cake.

Hannah slowly walked back to Aunt Millie's bedroom. She didn't know what to expect. Aunt Millie was a total stranger. She didn't even know that she had an Aunt Millie until a few days ago. A phone call came and the next thing she knew she was on a car ride half-way across the country.

"Come in dear," said Aunt Millie. "Come sit right next to me. Don't worry. You won't catch what I have."

"I know," said Hannah. "Mother told me it was your heart. But, I have to be careful you don't catch anything from me."

"Do you have anything slow enough for me to catch?" smiled Aunt Millie.

Hannah smiled back. It seemed Aunt Millie had a sense of humor. Hannah noticed a little gleam in the old woman's eyes. It was like she had a really good secret that she couldn't wait to tell.

"I don't think I have anything," said Hannah, "but you know kids are always getting things like colds, measles, and chicken pox. Mother says it doesn't always show up right away."

"You are so thoughtful," commented Aunt Millie. "The villagers are going to love you."

Hannah assumed Aunt Millie was talking about her neighbors. How wrong could Hannah be? Had she known what she would soon encounter, she would have thought quite differently about her aunt. She would have had a million questions.

Instead, she was already thinking of a polite way to excuse herself. Here she was in the presence of one of the most fascinating people she could ever hope to meet, and she didn't realize it. Hannah would look back at this time and think how foolish she had been to think so little of Aunt Millie. There's nothing like a great adventure to change your whole outlook on life.

Chapter 4

As the Ball Bounces

As Hannah sat on the edge of Aunt Millie's bed she became more bored. She listened to the rattling of pans coming from the kitchen.

"Sounds like your mom is cooking up something good in the kitchen," commented Aunt Millie. "I bet your mother is quite the cook."

Hannah pulled the red and yellow ball from her pocket. "Who does this belong to?"

Aunt Millie took the ball. "I haven't seen this in years. It belonged to my son Teddy. He used to have so much fun with it. His father gave it to him the day Teddy was born."

Aunt Millie smiled as she remembered. "He used to play fetch with his dog."

"What kind of dog did he have?" asked Hannah.

"He didn't have a dog," answered Aunt Millie.

The old woman noticed the confused look on Hannah's face. She smiled. Aunt Millie knew she had created more questions than answers. She handed the ball back to Hannah.

"See the teeth marks," Aunt Millie pointed to the little gray dots on the ball.

Hannah noticed them for the first time. "Did Teddy bite it?"

"No," laughed Aunt Millie. "Teddy had a pretend dog. It bit it. Teddy had such a fine pretend dog. It wasn't anything special in most people's eyes. Well, of course," laughed Aunt Millie, "nobody can actually see a pretend dog with their eyes. But, if they could, they would not be impressed with Fuzzbundle. He was a mutt, a little bit of this, a little bit of that. Yet old Fuzzbundle was everything a boy could want in a dog. He was brave, smart, playful, and above all, loyal."

"Wait," interrupted Hannah. "How can a pretend dog be all those things?" She held out the ball. "How can a pretend dog leave teeth marks on a real ball?"

"It just takes a little imagination," explained Aunt Millie as she took the ball back from Hannah, "and you can have any pretend dog of your choosing. Now about the teeth marks, it only takes a few drops of paint. Sometimes it's nice to tie our imaginations to something that is real. It's like connecting two different worlds."

"Teddy used to play fetch with Fuzzbundle for hours on end. Just like this," said Aunt Millie.

She tossed the ball right out of her room. Hannah was a little surprised. Her mom didn't like her throwing things in the house. Obviously, the rules were a little different in Aunt Millie's home. Hannah heard the ball bouncing off unknown objects as it traveled down the hall. For a sick old lady, Aunt Millie had quite an arm.

Hannah's mother stepped through the doorway carrying a tray of food. "What have I told you about throwing things in the house, young lady?"

"Nobody has called me a young lady in a very long time," chuckled Aunt Millie.

Hannah giggled. "Don't worry mom, Fuzzbundle will bring it back."

"Fuzzbundle?" questioned Hannah's mother. "What have you two been talking about? Are you filling Aunt Millie's mind with a lot of silly nonsense."

"No she's not," defended Aunt Millie. "I'm filling her head with nonsense, and not a bit of it is silly. It's very practical nonsense, useful in every way."

Hannah chewed on a sandwich as she enjoyed the conversation. Aunt Millie seemed to be a lot of fun. Hannah hoped she got well soon, so they could have even more fun. Then, she realized that she would go back home when Aunt Millie was well. Now she didn't know if she wanted Aunt Millie to get well quickly or slowly. Hannah pondered what to hope for as she finished eating.

"I thought Fuzzbundle would be back with that ball by now," sighed Aunt Millie after she took the last bite of her lunch. "Hannah, why don't you go and see what is keeping the old mutt? Sometimes he likes to play hide and seek with the ball, instead of fetch. I'll take a nap while you're gone."

Hannah left the room. She didn't think it would be too tough to find the rubber ball. She looked up the hall. She looked down the hall. There was no sign of the red and yellow ball. Hannah half-expected a big, fluffy mutt to come bounding down the hall with a drool covered ball in its mouth.

Most of the doors in the hallway were closed. One door was slightly ajar. Hannah judged that it was opened enough for the ball to roll through. Hannah slowly opened the door, checking for pretend dogs. The room was dark.

Hannah found a light switch. It turned on a lamp that sat on a small table. The room still seemed dimly lit. She wished she had a flashlight. Then she noticed the windows.

Heavy curtains were drawn closed. A small sliver of light peeked through. Hannah pulled them back. Suddenly, the room became much brighter and much more cheery.

She looked around. The walls were covered with shelves. Books were stacked on the shelves, but not the normal way. The books were stacked on top of each other. It all looked quite disorganized.

A small fireplace was in the room. Above the fireplace was a painting. The background of the painting was Aunt Millie's house in the spring time. There were all kinds of trees and blooming flowers. It looked quite delightful. Sitting on the front steps of the house was a young boy and a big, fluffy dog.

Hannah had forgotten all about the ball at this point. She was into exploring. Hannah loved to read, and all the books looked very old and interesting. As she walked around the room she found one shelf with books arranged differently then all of the others. She picked up one. It had a colorful cover and wonderful old illustrations on the inside. It must have been one of Teddy's books. She could imagine that it was his favorite.

One book looked plain next to the others. It had a worn, black cover. Hannah bent close and read the title: *The Room Upstairs*. She reached for the book and tried to pull it off the shelf.

The book didn't budge. Hannah wondered if someone had glued it to the shelf. She tugged again. Nothing happened. She was starting to get frustrated. She braced her foot on the wood paneling on the wall beneath the shelf. She placed both hands on the top, back corner of the book.

Suddenly, the book tilted forward, but it didn't come off the shelf. Hannah tumbled to the floor. The book snapped back into place. Hannah heard something moving in the room.

She turned around. A small section of the wall had slid behind a bookshelf. The small passageway revealed a narrow, curving staircase. The passageway was covered with dust and cobwebs. It was obvious that nobody had used it in years. Hannah looked back at the plain looking book. She read the title again, *The Room Upstairs*. For the first time she read the rest of the spine of the book: story by Teddy, pictures by Millie.

Chapter 5

The Room Upstairs

The spiral stairway was narrow, dusty, and full of cobwebs, yet it wasn't all that spooky. The walls were curved, so it was impossible to see where it led by looking up from the library. There was plenty of light in the stairway that Hannah guessed came from a window somewhere along the stairwell.

The cobwebs didn't look very inviting. Suddenly she remembered a small broom in the pantry. Hannah left the library and hurried down the hallway to the kitchen. She grabbed the broom on the back of the door. It had a small leather strap threaded through a hole in the top of the handle that allowed it to be hung on a hook. As Hannah pulled it off, she heard a clanking sound. Hanging on a second hook was a string with a bunch of old keys hanging on it. Hannah took the broom and made her way back to the hidden stairway.

Although it slowed down her exploring, Hannah was willing to clean her way to the top of the stairway. She felt like a jungle explorer hacking through thick vegetation as she cleared away the cobwebs.

Half-way up was a small window. Hannah looked out a dusty windowpane. She could see the outside world below her. She thought back to the morning when she wished she could have gotten out of the old house and play in the yard. Now, it all seemed kind of dull compared to the mysterious stairway she was climbing.

She looked up the stairwell. It grew darker as the light from the window faded. Hannah felt just a tinge of fear, but it wasn't enough to overcome her curiosity. She began cleaning again until she reached the top of the stairway.

The light was now very dim. At the top of the stairs was a small landing, a place to stand in front of a door. The door was small, almost child-sized. Hannah reached out to the brass doorknob and turned it. The door didn't open. Suddenly, she realized it was locked.

Hannah sat down on the landing and sighed. All that cleaning was wasted. If only she had a key. Suddenly, Hannah popped up. She remembered the keys on the rope hanging on the back of the pantry door. She rushed down the stairway and back to the pantry.

She pulled the string off the hook and wore the keys as a necklace. By now, she was so excited she was running. That was a bad idea. Loud, happy feet drew attention. Hannah had her mom's full attention as she rushed down the hallway.

"Hannah, come back here," said her mom in that voice that let Hannah know she had no other choice but to obey. Hannah sighed and slumped back down the hallway.

"You know better than to run inside," Hannah's mom waved her index finder at her. Then she noticed the keys. She took them in her hand and studied them.

"These are not something for you to play with. What if you misplaced them? These are probably very important. I'll take them for now."

"But, Mom," Hannah protested, maybe a little too loudly.

"Is there a problem?" asked Aunt Millie.

"It's these keys," Hannah's mother began to explain. "Hannah found them somewhere. I wouldn't want her to lose them."

"Bring them here," said Aunt Millie.

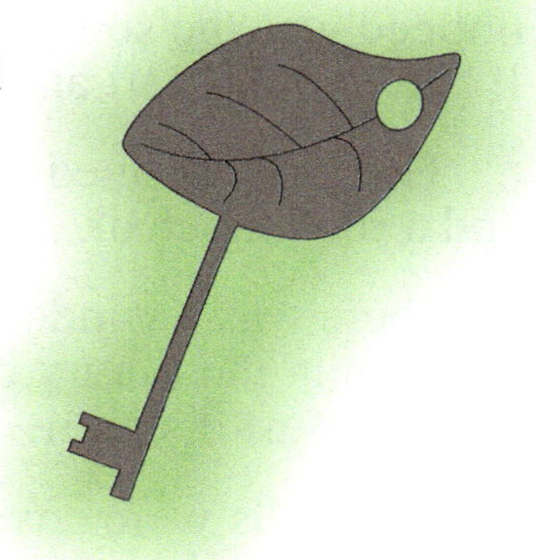

Hannah obeyed. She took the string off her neck and handed them to the old lady in the bed. Aunt Millie sorted through the keys. They were the old kind. They looked like small rods with flags on the ends. Each key had a different shape on the end that the key ring passed through. She found the smallest key and pulled it off the key ring. The key had a leaf on the end of it.

"This is the one you need, Dear," said Aunt Millie as she handed the key to Hannah. The old woman yawned. "Now, back to my nap."

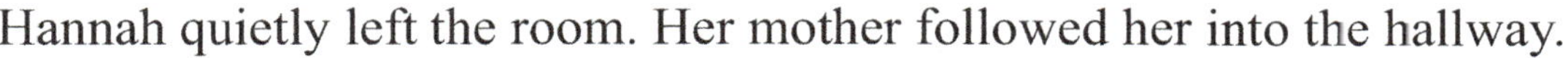

Hannah quietly left the room. Her mother followed her into the hallway.

"Just what are you up to?" asked Hannah's mother.

"I was cleaning," explained Hannah careful not to tell her too much about what was going on just in case her mother wouldn't approve. "I got the broom from the pantry. The keys were hanging on the same hook as the broom. They look pretty interesting, don't they?"

"You were cleaning?"

"Just some cobwebs and dust," answered Hannah.

Her mother smiled. "That's very good of you. Thank you for trying to do something useful." She glanced back at Aunt Millie. "I guess Aunt Millie doesn't have a problem with it. She gave you a key."

"Go on, but don't run anymore in the house. We're guests here. Put the broom back where you got it when you're finished and bring the key back."

Hannah smiled. She waited for her mother to go back into Aunt Millie's room. As soon as she was out of sight, Hannah zipped back to the staircase. She ran up the narrow steps to the small door.

The small key was in her hand. It looked like just the right size to work. The key hole looked like a circle with a rectangle on the bottom. That was the first time Hannah thought about the strange way Aunt Millie picked out the key. She didn't ask what Hannah wanted the keys for.

Hannah placed the key into the lock under the doorknob. She heard the click. Taking a deep breath, she pulled open the door. The hinges creaked from lack of use. Who knows when the last person entered the room? She expected more cobwebs.

The room was clean. There was no dust or cobwebs. Hannah looked around the room. Surely there was another doorway somewhere. There had to be a place where someone could come in and clean the room.

It was dark, so it took a few seconds for Hannah's eyes to adjust. The first thing she noticed was the strange shape of the room. It was not unlike the shape of the keyhole. It had a round part and a rectangle part.

The room seemed like a child's room, but there were no toys. There was a small bed and a rocking chair. Against one wall was a small set of drawers.

There was a window well seat under the window. The curtains made the room dark, just like in the library below. Hannah pulled them back. That's when she noticed the room's most distinctive feature.

The walls were covered by the most unusual wallpaper she had ever seen. It was mostly green. It was painted as a deep dark jungle. Thick tropical leaves and a few colorful flowers dotted the outside edges of the tropical forest scene. The walls had a depth to them. It was like you could have stepped right into it.

The more she looked, the heavier her eyes felt. Maybe all the cleaning and excitement wore her out. In one sense, it was all a let down. She had expected to find some spectacular treasure or at least some fun antique toys. Suddenly, the most inviting part of the room began to look like the small bed. Hannah wanted to lie down and just take a short nap.

Chapter 6

Inside the Closet

Hannah wasn't sure if she had slept for hours or just a few minutes. A sound in the room woke her. It wasn't a loud sound. Something was pressing against the closet door. Then it stopped.

Hannah listened intently as her heart started racing. She expected something to burst through the door at any moment. The door rattled again. This time it had a more familiar sound. It sounded like the wind. Aunt Millie's house must be drafty.

Hopping out of the bed, Hannah glanced out the window. Outside was a strange sight. The trees in the yard were not moving. There was no breeze, except for in the closet. Part of Hannah wanted to run downstairs, but she wanted to have courage.

Cautiously she approached the closet. The room grew darker as she stepped away from the window. Step by step she approached the closet door. It was now just a few inches in front of her.

She leaned her ear against the door. Sure enough, it sounded like a breeze. Suddenly, Hannah jumped back. There was a familiar sensation on her feet. She jumped back onto the edge of the bed.

Her hand felt the sock. It was soaked. She pulled off the socks and walked back to the door. Sure enough there was water seeping under the door. At first, Hannah thought there must be some broken water pipe in the closet.

Then, she noticed how strangely the water was behaving. It seeped under the door, and then it seeped back. Sometimes the water seeped all the way back to her heels. Other times it seeped only to her toes. Hannah had to make a decision.

Hannah was afraid; then she remembered what her mother taught her about courage. She wanted to do the right thing despite the fear. There could be something seriously wrong with Aunt Millie's house. It was up to her to discover what was happening.

She reached for the closet doorknob and slowly turned it. The closet was dark. Hannah reached out her hands to try to touch the back of the closet. She felt nothing.

Blindly she took a step. She was surprised that the floor of the closet was not hard wood like the floor of the room. Instead, it was soft and squishy. Something gritty oozed between her toes.

Her arms flailed hoping to reach the back of the closet. Still, she felt nothing. Carefully, she took another step. The water was now up to her ankles.

Another step and the water hit midway up her shin then dropped back to her ankle. With the next step, the water was nearly up to her knees and she still could not find any of the walls in the closet.

This was too strange. She suddenly decided it was time to turn back. She turned around and saw the doorway. As she started to walk back, the breeze picked up again. The door slammed shut.

"I picked a terrible time to finally have courage," she sighed.

The closet was totally dark and the water was splashing higher on her legs. Hannah wanted to run, but she didn't want to suddenly hit a wall. She controlled her fear and started carefully back to where she thought the door was.

Something brushed against her face. Instinctively she swiped at it with her arm. Something wrapped around her wrist. Hannah was caught by some kind of string. As she tried to jerk her arm away she heard a click.

A light was on above her head. For the first time, she could see inside the closet. Hannah couldn't believe her eyes. The closet looked larger then the whole house.

In fact, it looked bigger than the whole neighborhood. Hannah could clearly see that she was standing on a beach. In front of her was the jungle scene that was painted on the wall of the strange little bedroom at the top of the spiral staircase.

What she couldn't see was the doorknob. In fact, she couldn't even see the door. Hannah looked up at the light bulb. It looked like what you would expect to see in the closet of an old house. With one exception; you wouldn't expect it to be hanging in the air attached to nothing at all.

Hannah thought she must be dreaming. She pinched herself to see if it hurt. It did. She wished she hadn't pinched so hard, but she really wanted to believe what was happening wasn't real. Maybe she just dreamed it hurt and she was really still dreaming. She didn't want to pinch herself again to find out.

At least she could see the jungle wall. Although, it was strange that the wall was painted the same on both sides; she knew that had to be the way out. She couldn't see the door, so her plan was to feel along the wall until she found the way out.

She reached the wall and stretched out her arms. They went right into the wall. Well, not exactly; the wall wasn't a wall. It was exactly the way it looked. The wall was now a jungle. The first thing she felt was a leaf.

By this time, everything was getting brighter. She turned around to see a sun peaking over the horizon above the water. As the sun rose, the light bulb faded. Hannah suddenly realized it was the only thing connecting her world to the jungle world.

She splashed through the water and tried to grab the string. Her fingers passed right through it. The light bulb disintegrated right before her eyes. At the edge of the water she stepped on something.

Hannah reached down and picked up the object. It was very familiar.

"There it is. How did it get here?" she said as she studied the red and yellow ball.

She was sure it was the same one Aunt Millie had tossed out of her room. There was one thing different. The tooth marks that were painted on were now real. Hannah felt the little holes.

Her thoughts were interrupted by a sound. The leaves were rustling. Something was running toward her from the forest. It was moving fast.

Hannah's eyes grew large. Her heart raced. There was no place to hide and nowhere to run. She backed away from the edge of the jungle.

All at once, an animal popped out of the jungle. It wasn't a lion or bear as she feared. It was a dog. Not a ferocious looking dog, just a plain ordinary looking dog. Hannah didn't know what to think.

Would the dog hurt her? Would the dog be good company? The dog didn't seem to notice her right away. It was sniffing along the beach. Suddenly, it picked up Hannah's scent and started running toward her.

It charged down the beach. Not knowing where to run, Hannah just froze in place. The dog ran to about two feet from her and suddenly stopped. The dog wagged from tail to tongue.

She didn't know what the dog wanted, but at least she was sure it didn't want to hurt her. The dog approached her. He nudged her hand with his nose. It was the hand that held the ball.

Now Hannah understood. The dog wanted the ball.

"Fuzzbundle?" asked Hannah.

The dog barked and jumped in response.

Chapter 7

A Fuzzbundle of Joy

Hannah held the ball out to Fuzzbundle. The dog wouldn't take it. She tossed it on the ground.

"There boy," she said.

The dog nudged it with its nose back toward her. Then it ran a few steps and turned back to look at her. The dog had a look of expectation in its eyes.

"Oh, I get it," said Hannah. "You want to play."

She picked the ball up and tossed it. The dog ran after it. Fuzzbundle brought the red and yellow ball back and dropped it at her feet. Hannah picked it up again. This time she threw it a little farther.

The dog raced after the ball, barking happily. Hannah had always wanted a dog, so it was fun. She played fetch with the dog for several minutes. Then, Hannah began to think again about how strange everything was. She was playing fetch with a dog on a sunny beach inside a small closet.

She was thinking about what to do next when she tossed the ball again. The door had to be somewhere. Maybe it was just past the leaves. Perhaps she got turned around and it was in some other direction.

Hannah turned around in circles, carefully scanning every direction. There was the ocean. There was the jungle. Where was the door? Then another thought came to her. Where was Fuzzbundle?

"Fuzzbundle!" shouted Hannah.

There was no answer. Hannah started feeling afraid again. The beach seemed very lonely. She didn't know where she was. She didn't know where to go.

"Fuzzbundle!" this time there was panic in her voice.

Suddenly, she felt something crawl onto her foot. Hannah jumped and screamed. Then, she realized it was a hermit crab. She had seen them in pet shops. They were so fascinating then, not so fascinating when you're panicked and all alone.

She looked around to make sure she wasn't going to step on some other animal. Hannah also wanted to make sure no other animal had any ideas about stepping on her. That's when she noticed the paw prints. Of course, Fuzzbundle would have left a trail she could follow.

Hannah began to track the dog. There were many Fuzzbundle prints in the sand. That wasn't too big of a problem. She only had to walk by the vegetation. She looked for the set of prints that went into the jungle and didn't come back out. She began in the direction of her last throw.

Soon she found a sandy path. Hannah was a bit relieved. She had dreaded just walking into the tall vegetation. It would have made it difficult to find paw prints. But, she was more worried about things she might find, like creepy snakes and bugs, or other creatures that might bite.

Still, she was afraid to leave the beach. The door had to be somewhere. The last thing she needed to do was to get lost. That thought almost made her laugh.

"Get lost? How can I get lost when I don't know where I'm at? Who would think I could get lost in a closet?"

"Fuzzbundle, are you in there?"

She heard a distant bark. Hannah sighed. She could try to call the dog back, but would that change anything? Maybe Fuzzbundle could lead her to someone who could help.

Hannah took a few steps down the path. She turned back to look at the beach. It was sunny and bright. Then she turned again to the path. The tall trees with thick, wide leaves blocked the sunlight on the path. Each step she would take would be a little darker.

If only Fuzzbundle was by her side, it would give her a little more comfort. She was undecided. The path was frightening. Hannah turned back toward the beach one more time. She started to head back when something moved between her feet. This time, it didn't startle her. The moving object gave her comfort.

It was the red and yellow ball. She picked it up. It was caked with dog slobber and sand. Still, it was almost as precious as a diamond to Hannah because she heard the panting behind her. She turned around slowly. A relieved smile spread across her face.

Fuzzbundle! You came back for me," she got down on a knee to greet the dog.

Hannah gave the dog a hug. The dog responded with a lick across her face. Hannah giggled. The dog stood up, signaling that it was time to move forward. He moved down the path and looked back.

"I must have courage," sighed Hannah as she tucked the ball into her pocket.

She followed Fuzzbundle. The sandy path soon grew harder with smooth rocks. It also steadily became steeper. Hannah kept focusing on her surroundings. She tried to remember any unusual features. She might need to find her way back to the beach. She also looked for any signs of other people.

Fuzzbundle kept a pretty fast pace. "Slow down," complained Hannah. "You have four feet. I only have two."

She took another step. Suddenly, the ground crumbled around her. Hannah began to sink. She lunged for a vine, just as the ground gave way.

Hannah found herself dangling in the air. She tried to clutch the vine with her feet to help push her back to the path. The vine was too short. It didn't even reach to her waist.

"Help!" Hannah cried hopelessly.

She stared up. Fuzzbundle was at the edge of the hole. He looked down at her curiously. His head tilted to one side, then the other. He seemed to be asking, "Why are you in that hole?"

"Get help, Fuzzbundle. I can't hold on forever!"

The dog turned around and ran off. Hannah dangled. She peered to her left, trying to see the bottom of the hole. All she could see below her was darkness. The vine was digging into Hannah's hands. Her fingers were tingling and starting to hurt.

If things weren't bad enough, something tickled the back of her knee. The first thing she thought of was a bat. That made her wiggle and sway. The movement caused the vine to snap.

Hannah screamed as she plunged into the darkness.

Chapter 8

Into the Darkness

Almost as quickly as Hannah fell, she stopped falling. In fact, she only fell a couple of inches. Fuzzbundle was right by her side. It was his fur that had tickled the back of her knee.

"How did you get in here?" Hannah asked Fuzzbundle.

Then she noticed the bright circle off to her right. Hannah had fallen into a cave. Fortunately, it was a part that was near the surface of the ground. There was an entrance that the dog had used.

Hannah was so relieved that she wasn't hurt. She was also happy there was a way out. She walked toward the light. The opening was small, but Hannah was too. She was sure she could easily squeeze through.

Just as she was about to crawl through, Fuzzbundle tugged on her shirt. He seemed to be pulling her back. Was there something dangerous outside? Hannah suddenly didn't feel too sure about leaving the cave.

She turned around to see if she could get a better idea of what Fuzzbundle wanted. That's when she noticed another light. This one was more yellow, not the bright sunlight from the hole beside her. The other light flickered.

At first Hannah thought it was being carried. Then, she realized the light was a flame. It was a torch supported by a few rocks. Fuzzbundle trotted toward the torch. He looked back, expecting her to follow.

The dog had kept her safe, so far. The torch was perhaps a good sign. There had to be people around. Animals don't light torches. Then Hannah hesitated. There was no telling what kind of creature lit the torch. She was, after all, in a mysterious land inside a closet.

Hannah started back to the cave entrance. Fuzzbundle whined softly, but didn't move. Hannah stopped.

"Alright," she sighed. "I'll follow."

Hannah grabbed the torch. The cave was a maze of tunnels. Fuzzbundle seemed to know right where to go. She hoped the dog would be able to lead her out again because she was totally lost.

Suddenly the dog stopped. Fuzzbundle hopped into a wooden box in the middle of the floor. Hannah didn't know what to do. She didn't want to walk ahead of the dog. She didn't want to stand in the middle of a cave. Was this all Fuzzbundle wanted, to find his doggy bed?

Hannah stood by the box. Fuzzbundle barked. He jerked his head in a motion that seemed to say, "get in".

"Why not?" said Hannah. "I am a little tired.

As soon has she sat down, the dog stretched out his neck. That was the first time Hannah noticed the rope. The dog clenched it in his teeth and pulled down.

Somewhere behind her, Hannah heard a loud whoosh. She turned around and stuck out the torch to see what made the sound. There was something moving down the tunnel. It seemed to be coming fast.

Suddenly, it appeared around the corner. A large wave of water was bearing down on them. Hannah wanted to run, but realized the water was moving a lot faster than she could.

In a second it had reached the box. Hannah and Fuzzbundle were lifted up and swept along by the wave. They twirled and floated down the tunnel. Hannah hung on tightly. They picked up speed as the box was swept from one drop off to another.

Hannah screamed as they went down, down into the cave. Fuzzbundle barked with joy. Hannah noticed how relaxed the dog was. He was having a great time.

Then, she realized the dog had somehow started the whole water raft ride by pulling the rope.

"You planned this!" shouted Hannah.

Fuzzbundle responded with a couple of happy barks and some satisfied panting.

Suddenly, the box splashed into a large underground lake. It slowed down and drifted.

"Now what?" Hannah asked the dog.

Fuzzbundle fished around the bottom of the box and pulled something up. Between his teeth was an oar. He laid it on Hannah's lap. He shook his head up and down and barked.

"This is your plan?" asked Hannah. "You set us adrift on this underground lake and want me to row."

Fuzzbundle barked yes.

"I don't even know where to row to," said Hannah. "Do you have any better ideas?"

The dog seemed to think again. After a few seconds he rummaged around the bottom of the boat again. This time he had a rope between his teeth.

Hannah thought the dog was going to give it to her again, expecting her to get out and pull the boat. Instead the dog dropped it over the side of the box. Fuzzbundle let out three short yips. Almost instantly something in the water began tugging the rope.

Hannah heard the whir of the rope. It was being quickly pulled over the edge of the box. Suddenly the rope tightened. It was tied to the box. The box began to move forward, slowly at first. Then, it began to pick up speed.

Hannah was a little worried. Maybe rowing wasn't such a bad idea. She didn't know what was at the end of the rope. Hannah leaned over the edge and held out the torch. Whatever was pulling them was under water.

She leaned a little further. At that moment, a large creature popped out of the water right in front of her nose. Hannah fell back into the box. As she looked up, the great creature jumped right over the box. With a great splash, it disappeared beneath the surface of the lake.

"What was that?" Hannah said out loud.

Just then, the creature popped up behind her and let out a strange sound. Hannah turned in terror. Then there was another animal to her right. All the time the box was traveling faster.

Hannah carefully lifted the torch, trying to see the ferocious underwater monsters. One popped up to her left. This time Hannah got a good look. It wasn't a terrifying creature after all. What she saw was a pure, white dolphin. The creature was beautiful and looked very friendly.

Chapter 9

The End of the Tunnel

A scraping sound on the bottom of the box let Hannah know the water was getting shallow. Fuzzbundle hopped from the box and splashed to shore. Hannah followed. When she reached land, she held the torch above her head and turned back to the lake. She saw three white dolphins. Hannah waved to them.

"Thank you," she yelled.

The dolphins squealed back to her, waved and disappeared below the surface of the lake. When Hannah turned around, Fuzzbundle was gone. There were three tunnels to choose from on the shore. Hannah waved the torch on the ground. Fuzzbundle had left a trail of drips to the middle tunnel.

Hannah followed. The tunnel started out very small. Hannah bent down as low as she could without crawling. Her eyes scanned the rocks above her. She didn't want to bump her head.

Gradually the tunnel got taller and wider. Hannah seemed to be walking uphill. That was a good sign in her mind. She hoped to get back to the surface sometime.

Hannah was surprised by what was at the end of the tunnel. Right before her eyes was a large, heavy looking, wooden door. It looked quite out of place in the middle of a cave. Hannah guessed that the only polite thing to do was to knock. The door looked so thick that she was sure not much of a knocking sound would emanate from the other side.

She decided to just try opening it. Maybe if there was something bad on the other side, she could close the door. Hannah pushed the knob. The door seemed to be locked or even rusted shut.

Then, Hannah thought of Fuzzbundle. She was at the end of the tunnel and there was no dog. Had she missed a tunnel on the way from the lake? Had she taken a wrong turn somewhere? She hadn't seen any other way Fuzzbundle could have come but this tunnel.

"Fuzzbundle!" Hannah called out.

Hannah heard a squeak down by her legs. The bottom of the door was moving. The heavy, wooden door had a doggy door in it. Fuzzbundle poked his head out and panted. Hannah got on her hands and knees to see the dog. She saw that she could easily fit through the doggy door. So, she crawled.

When she got to her feet on the other side, she found herself in a very large space. In the center of the space was a pool of water. About fifty feet above the pool was an opening in the ceiling. Hannah was comforted seeing the shaft of sunlight.

There were tiny grass huts in the space. It looked like some kind of a village. The floor was painted green with gray and brown paths. Clouds and a blue sky were even painted on the high ceiling. Hannah thought at first there were flowers and trees. Then she noticed they were painted pieces of wood shaped like plants.

Beyond the pool of water was a large curtain. Curved steps from each side of the curtain were carved out of the rock. There didn't appear to be any people around, which was good. Hannah wanted to explore.

The huts were interesting. She started toward one. Fuzzbundle barked and walked toward the steps. Hannah decided to follow the dog once again. Fuzzbundle stopped at the bottom of the steps. Hannah stopped behind him.

That didn't satisfy the dog. He stood to the side of the stairway. He put a paw on the first step. The dog looked at Hannah, and then turned his head to look up the stairs.

"You want me to go first?" asked Hannah.

The dog shook his head, yes. Hannah stepped onto the first step. She put her hand on the wall to steady herself. The step was not solid. It wobbled a little. Hannah stepped off and stood next to Fuzzbundle. The dog began to whine.

"It's not safe," Hannah tried to explain. "The step is wobbly."

Fuzzbundle rested his chin on the step. He looked up at Hannah. The dog looked so sad and disappointed. Hannah sighed.

"Ok, I'll try again."

Hannah steadied herself against the wall as she climbed the first step. It still wobbled. Hannah paused and took a deep breath. She stepped on the next step. It was firm and didn't wobble at all. Hannah was relieved. The next two steps were firm too, and Hannah gained more confidence.

Then, Hannah stepped on the fifth step. It seemed to sink a little. Hannah thought she heard a click sound. That frightened her. She looked back at Fuzzbundle. He had both front paws on the first step. He waved his head as if to encourage her along.

Hannah took the sixth step. Nothing happened. She took the next three steps without noticing anything unusual. There were now only three more steps to the top.

As soon as she stepped on the tenth step it began to move into the wall. She quickly hopped onto the eleventh step. It started moving in too, only faster. Hannah now ran up the twelfth step and stepped onto the platform. The twelfth step zipped into the wall behind her, followed by all the other steps on both sides of the platform.

Fuzzbundle was below her. He had not climbed the steps. The dog didn't seem the least bit upset that Hannah was trapped.

"Thanks, Fuzzbundle," said Hannah sarcastically.

The only place left to go was behind the curtain. She wished she could open the curtain, but she couldn't find a rope to pull. In fact, she had a difficult time finding an opening. She felt along the thick, red velvety curtain until she got to the center.

Hannah held it back to let the light in. Behind the curtain was a small stage. At the back of the stage was a single chair. It was very ornate. It looked like it was covered with gold and jewels.

She recognized that it was some kind of throne. It was a rather small throne. The chair looked just the right size for a child, like her. It was just too tempting. Hannah had to sit on it. She slipped behind the curtain.

As the flap closed, the stage became much darker. Hannah regretted not bringing a torch. Still, there was enough light to see the throne. She carefully walked toward it.

There were three small steps leading up to the throne. Hannah kept her arms outstretched as she climbed them, prepared to stumble. As she put her hand on one of the arms of the chair, she expected to feel the precious gems. Instead the arm was smooth.

Hannah sat down on the throne. Although the throne was hard, it sunk a bit when Hannah sat on it. Suddenly she heard a rumbling sound behind her. The throne began to shake. Slowly, the curtain started to open.

At the same time, the whole stage seemed to slide backward. Hannah was frightened, but didn't know what to do. She gripped the arms of the throne tightly and closed her eyes.

Chapter 10

The Brave One

After a few minutes, everything stopped moving. Hannah opened her eyes. The first thing she noticed was that the jeweled throne was simply painted to look like jewels. The next thing she noticed was that there was now a wide set of steps in front of her.

It was like they unfolded like the bleachers in the school gym. Fuzzbundle trotted up the steps. He practically jumped in her lap and licked her face. The dog seemed overjoyed.

The throne wasn't the only thing that moved. All the huts had moved back. In fact, they were all huddled in one corner of the cave. The door on one of the huts slowly opened. Hannah saw someone peek out. A small figure dashed out and hid behind a boulder.

"Who's there?" asked Hannah.

She saw two eyes peek over the boulder.

"I won't hurt you," Hannah coaxed. "Don't be afraid."

The head jerked back quickly. Hannah had an idea. She pulled the red and yellow ball from her pocket.

"Would you like to play catch?" asked Hannah as she held up the ball.

"My ball," said the voice.

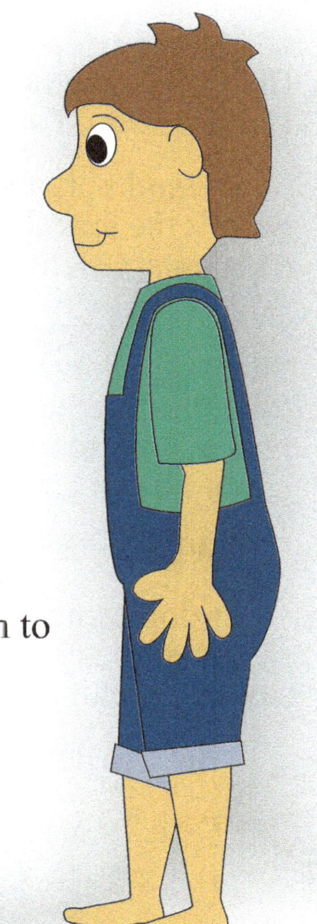

A young boy ran from behind the rock to the bottom of the steps.

"May I have it back? I've been looking all over for it," said the boy in a soft voice.

The boy looked a little younger than Hannah. He was dressed in clothes that Hannah thought looked very old fashioned. He wore bib overalls and a t-shirt. It looked quite out of place for a tropical island.

"Sure," said Hannah. "Come and get it."

The boy hesitated a minute. Slowly he climbed the steps. His eyes never left Hannah. At the top of the steps, he stared at the floor as he approached the throne. After looking at the ball, Hannah began to wonder something.

"Are you Teddy?" asked Hannah.

"Yes, your majesty," answered the boy. "Do you know me?"

"I know your mother," answered Hannah.

The boy looked up. "I have a mother?"

Oh boy, thought Hannah. She wished she had never mentioned Aunt Millie. The boy's mother had grown old. Teddy had not changed. That was more than Hannah could explain.

"Maybe I'm thinking of someone else," said Hannah.

"I know who you are," said the boy.

"You do?" said Hannah.

She was surprised, but at this point she thought anything was possible. "What's my name?"

"The Brave One!" Teddy exclaimed.

His voice echoed off the walls of the cavern. The huts started moving again. They shifted back to their original spots. One by one, the doors began to creak open. Slowly people started stepping out the doors.

They walked slowly to the foot of the platform. The people were very small. They didn't seem to be much bigger than Hannah. They wore ragged clothes, nothing colorful at all.

They were whispering to one another and pointing at Hannah. After awhile, Hannah began to understand what they were saying. They were repeating the words of Teddy. The people were calling Hannah The Brave One.

"Why are you calling me that?" asked Hannah.

All the people started pointing back at her. At least, that's what Hannah thought at first. Then she noticed that they were all pointing above her head. For the first time, Hannah turned around.

Behind her, above the throne, was a large painting. It was about ten feet high. It wasn't the size that amazed Hannah; it was the subject of the painting. It was a picture of Hannah. Below the picture were the words, The Brave One.

Below the painting was a door. Hannah could see sunlight beaming from under it. She would have raced through the door a short time ago. Now, she wasn't quite ready to leave. She had too many questions about the mysterious underground room and the people who seemed to live there. Most of all, she had a big question about the big picture behind her.

"When was that picture painted?" Hannah asked Teddy.

"I don't know," answered Teddy. "The curtain has never been opened. The legend says that the curtain will only open for The Brave One. Today is the first time we ever saw the picture."

"But I'm not brave," protested Hannah. "I'm not brave at all. I'm scared of everything."

"Perhaps you can be both scared and brave," said Teddy.

“You are beginning to sound like my mother,” sighed Hannah. “You said there is a legend. What is The Brave One supposed to do? Am I supposed to just sit on the throne all day?”

“The Brave One has come to save us,” said Teddy. “Your courage will rescue us from the angry Chief Honcho. He banished us to this cave. Only you can save us and take us back to the land with the sky.”

“How long have you lived in this cave?” asked Hannah.

“Centuries,” cried out one of the people.

“Thousands of years,” someone else corrected.

“Since the beginning of time,” said another.

Soon the people were arguing about how long they had lived in the cave. Everyone seemed to have a different answer. Finally, Teddy stuck two fingers in his mouth. He whistled very loudly.

“Let’s ask Father Timekeeper,” said Teddy.

The people murmured in agreement. Someone from the back of the crowd ran to a hut. A second later the person emerged leading a small, old man. He had a long gray beard. He wore a brown robe. Around his neck was a clock like one you would see on a wall. Under his arm was a thick book.

The crowd parted as he walked to the steps. Two young men helped him climb the first two steps.

“You have a question for Father Timekeeper?” asked the old man.

Teddy walked down to him.

“We were wondering how many centuries, decades, or years our people have lived in the cave,” said Teddy. “Can you give us an answer?”

“I see,” said Father Timekeeper.

The old man sat down on the step. He began to flip through the thick book. Father Timekeeper found the page he was looking for. He placed the book on the step. Then he looked at the clock.

Next, Father Timekeeper pulled out a pad of paper and a pencil from the pocket of his robe. He began to write down some numbers. The old man looked at his notes thoughtfully.

“Add the four. Carry the one,” Father Timekeeper mumbled as he calculated. “I have it!” he finally announced.

The crowd leaned in, waiting for the answer.

“Nine years!” announced Father Timekeeper.

“That sounds about right,” murmured the crowd.

Chapter 11

Into the Daylight

Just then, a loud commotion broke out behind the people. Objects were falling from the hole at the top of the cavern. They landed with a splash in the water. Hannah noticed that they were coconuts. The people grabbed nets and fished the food out of the pool.

Next, a bucket was lowered. It was full of carrots.

"What was that?" asked Hannah.

"It's the provider. He throws food down once a week," explained Teddy.

"He's two minutes early this week," said Father Timekeeper.

"So this is all you get to eat, carrots and coconuts?" asked Hannah.

"We get water, too," said someone from the crowd.

"That's not much of a life," said Hannah. "Why don't you leave? Oh, I forgot you were waiting for The Brave One. Okay, I'm here now, so let's leave. There's a door right behind the throne."

Hannah walked to the door. She opened it up. Sure enough, it was a stairway to the bright, sunny outdoors. She expected everyone to climb the steps up to the throne. Instead, nobody moved.

"Let's go," said Hannah. "Let's get out of here."

"You go," said the people. "You're The Brave One."

Hannah sighed, "Okay, I'll go, but someone needs to lead the way."

The room grew silent. All the people looked away. Hannah was beginning to feel like she was the only brave one. Finally, Fuzzbundle trotted up to the door. Hannah saw Teddy peek around the throne. He was trying to get the dog's attention. Teddy had a worried look on his face. He was motioning for the dog to come to him.

Hannah put her arm around the dog, "If you want to stay near Fuzzbundle, you'll just have to come with us."

She was getting a little upset that nobody would take a chance. They all depended on her to be brave. Teddy felt a little ashamed. He slowly inched toward Hannah and Fuzzbundle.

"You go first," said Teddy as he motioned to the stairs.

"Are you afraid?" asked Hannah.

"I am just being polite," said Teddy.

Fuzzbundle took the lead. The children ran up the stairs after him. Although Hannah felt safer in the cave, she was very glad to be back in the sunlight. She squinted her eyes because of the brightness.

Behind her was the entrance to the cave. It was on the side of a mountain. Hannah thought she heard thunder. That was strange. There wasn't a cloud in the sky. The rumbling grew louder. She looked back at the mountain.

"Run!" she screamed.

Teddy, Fuzzbundle, and Hannah ran along a path. They ducked behind a very large boulder. The three huddled together as rocks flew over and around them. When it grew quiet, Hannah peeked over the boulder. An avalanche had covered the entrance to the cave.

"There's no going back now," said Hannah. "Which direction should we go to find Chief Honcho?"

"I don't have any idea," said Teddy.

Hannah was upset, "What do you mean you don't have any idea? You came along to lead the way."

Teddy stared at the ground and kicked at the dirt. "I thought you would tell me which way to go. Then I would lead the way. I've never been above ground before."

Hannah looked around. To the left was a jungle. To the right was more of the jungle. Ahead of them was a cliff with a pool of water below.

"Let's go to the left," said Hannah.

Hannah turned to walk into the jungle.

"Duck!" cried Teddy.

Hannah ducked just as something flew over her head. She saw a spear hit the trunk of a tree.

"Run!" cried Hannah as she ran more quickly toward the jungle.

"Stop!" cried Hannah when she saw warriors running right toward her.

Fuzzbundle barked and ran to the edge of the cliff. Hannah and Teddy followed. Hannah looked below at the pool of water. Teddy started crying.

"I'm afraid," said Teddy. "I can't jump."

At that moment, warriors came from the jungle from both sides. They carried spears and were ready to attack. There was no time to waste.

"Teddy, have courage. Jump on three. One…two…three!"

Hannah jumped. She had never been so frightened in her life. The pool grew closer. She hoped it was deep enough for such a dive. Out of the corner of her eye she saw Fuzzbundle falling beside her.

She squeezed her eyes tight, took a deep breath, and prepared for the impact. Hannah felt her body hit something, but it was not water. She opened her eyes to see that she was no longer falling. In fact, she soaring into the sky.

Fuzzbundle was still beside her. The dog was soaring upward too. He seemed to thoroughly enjoy the ride. In a second, they flew above the edge of the cliff.

Hannah caught a glimpse of the warriors. Two warriors had Teddy by the arms. He was swinging his legs, trying to get away. Then, Hannah and Fuzzbundle started falling again.

By now, Hannah had realized that the pool of water was actually a trampoline. This time when Hannah and the dog landed, Fuzzbundle did somersault. He barked with happily in satisfaction. Hannah had to giggle.

It took a few minutes, but slowly the bouncing diminished. Hannah and Fuzzbundle were able to finally stop bouncing. Hannah slipped off the edge. Her knees were wobbling. Her body was still anticipating a bounce.

Hannah was unsure of what to do first. Should she find Chief Honcho? If she found him what would she do? Now, she was even more unsure. Teddy needed rescuing. She was just a little girl. How could she face the warriors?

Fuzzbundle sensed her confusion. He hopped from the trampoline and began to lead the way. At that moment, Hannah was happy not to have to make the decision. She followed the dog into the forest.

Chapter 12

The Return of the Door

Fuzzbundle ran along the path. Hannah stayed right on his tail. Suddenly the dog stopped. Hannah walked up next to the dog. At its feet was a hole in the pathway. Hannah recognized it as the one she had fallen into.

The dog carefully walked around it and got back onto the path. Hannah followed. Things started looking familiar to Hannah. Fuzzbundle was leading her back to the beach.

In a few minutes, she could hear the water hitting the shore. The ground beneath her feet became soft and sandy. Hannah and Fuzzbundle emerged from the jungle. It was the same beach.

The dog started running along the edge of the water. Hannah didn't follow. She saw something to her left. A slight breeze was blowing. The leaves of the plants around her rocked gently in the wind.

Yet, the plants ahead of her to her left were perfectly still. Hannah thought it was strange. She walked toward them. Could it be?

Hannah reached out to touch them. Her suspicion was confirmed. They weren't plants, but a wall. It was the closet wall. She felt along the wall until she found what she was looking for.

Her hand caught the doorknob. She turned it. The door opened. Ahead of her was the small bed in the upper room of Aunt Millie's house. Hannah felt such a great relief. She started to step through when she heard a soft whine behind her.

Hannah turned around to see Fuzzbundle. The dog had such a sad look on its face. He looked away from her and started to slowly walk away down the beach. Suddenly, her relief turned to sorrow. Teddy needed help. The people needed to be freed from the cave.

Hannah looked at the safety of the room. She thought about the danger on the island. Hannah thought again about what her mother had said about courage. She was afraid, but there was a right thing to do that required her to act in spite of the fear.

She slammed the door. Instantly, the plants on the wall began to sway in the breeze. Hannah reached out again. All she felt was more of the jungle. After letting out a heavy sigh, Hannah ran after Fuzzbundle.

When the dog heard her, he turned. Fuzzbundle hopped up on her. His paws rested on her shoulders as he licked her face. He was as playful as the first time they met in about the same spot. Fuzzbundle ran around Hannah, and then trotted down the beach. Hannah followed.

She was glad they weren't going back into the jungle. The dog was leading her around a corner. Soon, the place with the door was out of sight. The beach grew less sandy and slimier. Seaweed had washed up on the beach. Hannah had to be careful not to slip.

The dog suddenly turned up a path in the jungle. Fuzzbundle led her to a door in a stone wall. Obviously, Fuzzbundle wanted her to go inside. Hannah started to knock on the door when she heard it unlatch.

The door slowly creaked open. Fuzzbundle walked right in. Hannah was more cautious. She pushed the door open a little farther. Inside she saw a large vegetable garden. Around the edges of the wall were all kinds of fruit trees.

"Hello," said Hannah.

She expected the person who opened the door to answer. No one was in sight. Then she noticed the rope above her head. It ran through a pulley and was tied to a latch on the door. Hannah stepped through the gateway. The first thing she saw was a sign.

"Please latch the door behind you. No warriors allowed."

Hannah definitely wanted to latch the door if it could keep out warriors. Fuzzbundle was nowhere in sight. Hannah looked at the rope overhead. It had to lead to the person who opened the door. The rope was attached to a hand crank on a post.

The post supported a tiny porch on a shed at the back of the garden. It had a tin roof and was nicely painted. A little shelf was mounted to the post about a foot below the hand crank.

Inside the shed were all kinds of gardening tools. There were rakes, hoes, watering cans, shovels, and more. Everything was neatly organized.

"Hello," yelled Hannah. "Thank you for letting me in. I am friendly."

Nobody answered. Suddenly, there was a loud thump on the roof of the shed. It was followed by a rolling sound. It sounded like a bowling ball. Hannah looked up in time to jump away.

A coconut landed at her feet. That gave Hannah an idea. She found an axe in the tool shed. Hannah chopped off the outer husk to reveal a smaller nut-like shell. She was getting hungry. She started to go back into the shed for a hammer.

Hannah stepped onto the porch. Suddenly, there was another thump on the roof. This time there was a sliding sound instead of a rolling sound. Then it stopped. Hannah looked above at the bottom of the porch's roof. Something alive was moving around.

A board creaked under her feet as she shifted her weight. A small hand swept down from the roof and knocked the coconut right out of her hand. It rolled onto the ground. A furry creature sprung from the roof and grabbed the coconut. Hannah ran into the shed and closed the door.

Outside Hannah could hear the animal bashing the coconut against a rock. When that sound stopped, she could hear the animal approach the door. There was a soft knock on the door. The knock seemed to come from the lower part of the door. There was a small window in the shed.

Hannah looked out the window. All she could see was a furry tale. She tried to get a better angle to see more of the animal. At that instant, a face looked back at her through the glass.

It was a smiling, monkey face. He held up half a coconut. The monkey carefully placed it on the window sill. The small creature hopped up on the platform by the hand crank. He had the other half of the coconut and was drinking the milk.

Carefully, Hannah opened the door. The monkey pointed at the shell on the window. Hannah took the shell. The monkey held its half to its mouth and drank. The small animal seemed to be trying to teach her how to use the shell.

Hannah giggled and took the shell. Most of the coconut water had spilled when it cracked open. Still, she appreciated what was there. After drinking, the two enjoyed a snack of the coconut meat.

Chapter 13

The Provider

"You *must* be the Brave One if you were able to take food away from Teeko."

The voice startled Hannah. A tall, thin man with white hair approached her with Fuzzbundle at his heels. The smiling man looked friendly. He reminded Hannah of her grandfather.

"He shared with me," Hannah explained.

"Indeed," said the man. "He knows who you are. Teeko wouldn't open the gate for just anyone."

"Where is everyone else?" asked Hannah.

"It's just Teeko and me," said the man. "Once in awhile, Fuzzbundle pays us a visit."

"You must eat a lot," Hannah commented.

The man laughed. "You noticed my garden. It's not all for Teeko and me."

Hannah made a connection, "You are the Provider!"

"The people of the cave call me that," said the man, "but I have a name. It is Joshua. I do wish you would call me that. It's so unusual to find someone friendly and brave."

"I'm not sure I'm so brave," said Hannah. "All I did was walk into a closet."

"I think you underestimate yourself," said Joshua. "Teeko is a good judge of character. If he thinks you are worthy of half his food, you *are* worthy."

Teeko shook his head yes in agreement. He came over and sat in her lap. The monkey handed her the rest of his coconut. Hannah gave the monkey a little hug. The monkey turned his head shyly, hunched his shoulder, and smiled.

Joshua stared at Hannah's face. He squinted a little. He cocked his head and stared some more.

"I've got to work on your nose," said Joshua.

Hannah felt her face. She rather liked her nose. It didn't feel like something that needed to be worked on. Then she thought of all the tools in the garden shed.

Joshua noticed the concerned look on her face.

"That's it!" he said. "That's the look I need to capture."

"I think I need to be going," Hannah said in a tense voice as she gently nudged Teeko from her lap.

"No, no!" Joshua began to explain. "I'm talking about the painting of you. I've been working on it for months and I just haven't been able to get it right."

"For months? I just got here. How could you have been painting me for months?"

"We've been expecting you for years," Joshua explained. "You are the Brave One. Remember the picture above the throne? I painted that one, too. It was a pretty good likeness, if I say so myself. The one in the Hall of History is from a different angle. I just couldn't picture the nose until now."

"May I see this picture?" asked Hannah.

"I insist," said Joshua. "Follow me to the Hall of History."

Hannah, Fuzzbundle, and Teeko followed Joshua up the path. Teeko took Hannah's hand and smiled. The path ended at what Hannah first thought was another cave; yet, it was different. The outside was smooth and shiny. It had brown stripes on it.

"This is an unusual looking cave," Hannah commented.

"It's not a cave," Joshua explained. "It's a giant nautilus shell. You might picture it as a giant snail shaped shell."

"In my world, shells don't get this big," said Hannah. "I've held a nautilus shell in my hand."

"Interesting," said Joshua. "The question is: are you smaller now or is the shell bigger?"

As Hannah pondered the question Joshua entered the shell. "Are you coming?"

Hannah ran after Joshua. The shell was huge. It seemed like a whole house could fit inside it. The first thing Hannah saw was a painting of her on the wall of the shell. She had to admit, Joshua didn't quite have the nose right.

Joshua climbed a scaffold and grabbed his paint pallet. He was anxious to fix the painting. Hannah watched from below as he painted.

"I think I have it now, Dear. Your nose is now perfect," said Joshua. "If you'd like to explore the Hall of History, I'd like to take you on the tour. I'm sure you would find it most interesting and maybe even helpful."

"I'm in sort of a hurry," Hannah explained. "You see, a little boy named Teddy has been captured by warriors. He needs my help."

"I'm well aware of Teddy's precarious predicament," said Joshua. "Can you tell me just how you plan to help him? Do you know where to find him?"

"No," answered Hannah. "I had hoped you could help me. I assumed that's why Fuzzbundle led me here."

“Yes,” said Joshua. “I can help you and I will. We must start with a history lesson.”

Joshua walked with Hannah deeper and deeper into the shell. As they walked the spiral pathway, the room got smaller and smaller. The walls were painted with scenes from the history of the island.

“Here is where the history of the cave people started,” Joshua explained. “Chief Alexander was the last of the royal chief line to rule the island. One day, he was sailing when a storm arose. His boat was swept to another island. His nearly lifeless body washed up on the beach.

When he awoke, the most beautiful face he had ever seen was looking down at him. He instantly fell in love. It turned out she was the daughter of the chief on that island. Her name was Millicent.

He married the chief’s daughter. Alexander was very worried about the people on his island. He wanted to return. Millicent’s father agreed. He gave him his finest boat. Two of his warriors knew the way back to Alexander’s island. Millicent’s father allowed them to go along as a guide.

That was a mistake. They brought rats with them back to the island and turned them loose in the food bin. Then, they kept everyone from seeing the chief. When they learned about the great beast of the forest, they lured it to the village. They trapped the beast in the village closet.

They threatened to throw anyone who didn’t obey them to the beast. Then, one day, Chief Alexander disappeared. Everyone assumed the chief had been eaten by the beast in the closet.

One of the warriors declared himself as chief. The other one became his captain. Soon, six other warriors arrived on the island. They terrorized the people. Anyone who spoke against them was threatened with the beast.

A short time later, Millicent had baby boy. She feared the warriors would kill the child because he was the rightful chief. She was too weak to travel, but some of the villagers snuck the child away, along with all the other children in the village. The warriors had planned to kill all the children, just to make sure the chief’s son died.

They hid away in a cave. The warriors never found them. When I discovered the cave people, they had almost starved to death. I tried to get them to leave the cave, but they were too afraid. I started feeding them, and have done so for nine long years.”

Hannah stared at the painting near the back of the shell. A beautiful young woman held a baby in her arms. Hannah’s jaw dropped when she saw what the baby was holding. It was the red and yellow ball.

“That’s Teddy’s ball!” said Hannah.

“Chief Theodore,” smiled Joshua.

“Does he know?” asked Hannah.

“No,” answered Joshua. “He won’t know until he finds the courage to be a chief. Then in his heart he will know. So will all the villagers.”

Chapter 14

The Village

"I do wish you would come with us," said Hannah the next morning as she began to start out to the village.

"And if something should happen to me, all the people of the cave would starve," explained Joshua. "You have the courage to see this through. See, I've almost finished the painting. Teeko will show you the way."

Hannah barely glanced at the painting. She was too concerned about rescuing Teddy. Now that she knew he was a chief, she was even more concerned. If she failed, the people of the cave may never enjoy a sunshiny day.

The monkey sat on Fuzzbundle's back. He clapped at the sound of his name. Then the monkey pointed toward the gate. Joshua gave Hannah a backpack full of carrots.

"You may need these."

Hannah took the backpack. She wasn't too excited about carrying all that weight. She already had large jug of water. Joshua saw the look of hesitation. He looked her in the eyes. A serious look was on his face.

"You will need these. They are your only defense," he said firmly.

"Don't you have a spear or maybe a rocket launcher?" asked Hannah. She was ready for more firepower than carrots.

"Courage and carrots are all you need," said Joshua.

"How about a cannon? It begins with c," suggested Hannah.

"You will make history today," Joshua encouraged Hannah.

"I never liked history," she mumbled.

Hannah started down the path. Joshua had made her a pair of sandals the night before. It was a good thing. The path was steep and rocky. By mid-day, they had reached the top of a mountain. It was the highest point on the island. There were no trees or tall plants.

The beach could be seen in every direction. It was beautiful, but also a little frightening. In the distance, Hannah could make out little puffs of smoke rising from cooking fires in the village. The pathway down the other side was narrow with steep drop-offs. One slip could be fatal.

By the afternoon, the path was getting less steep and wider. Soon, they were back in a jungle. Teeko was still directing the way. Occasionally, they would have to stop. The monkey would climb to the top of a tree and scout out the way.

Within an hour, they were hiding at the edge of the village. Warriors were watching over the villagers. They were forcing them to do work. The villagers carried food into Chief Honcho's hut.

A woman carrying a large basked of fruit walked near them. She was followed by a warrior. She tripped on a stone and the basket spilled. The warrior started yelling at her. She picked up some of the fruit. When she looked up, she saw Hannah.

The woman looked worried. She quickly gathered up the rest of the fruit and hurried to Chief Honcho's hut. When she came back out, she grabbed a rake. She worked her way back to the edge of the jungle.

She looked away from Hannah. The woman didn't want to draw any attention to what she was doing. She sang softly like someone trying to stay entertained while working. Hannah thought it was strange until she began to listen to the words the woman was singing.

"The boy is in the hut in the middle of the village. The chief is going to burn him at the stake very shortly."

The woman didn't notice the warrior that had come up behind her. The warrior listened. Soon he joined in singing.

"The boy is in the hut in the middle of the village. The chief is going to burn him at the stake very shortly."

The woman turned around. The warrior was smiling.

"That's a very nice song. I like it," said the warrior.

The woman laughed nervously, "thank you." She quickly raked herself away from Hannah and the animals.

Hannah looked over the village. It seemed like there were warriors watching everything. In the middle of the village, a hut was being guarded by a large warrior with an even larger spear. There was no way Hannah could sneak around the village. She had hoped to wait until nighttime, but Teddy may not make it until then.

"What we need is some kind of diversion," Hannah said to Teeko and Fuzzbundle.

The monkey rubbed his chin thoughtfully as he sat on the dog's back. Suddenly, he slapped Fuzzbundle on the thigh. The dog twisted his head around with a snarl on his face. The dog's face relaxed. He understood before Hannah.

Fuzzbundle shot out of the brush. Teeko rode on his back. The dog raced to a warrior and grabbed a spear in his teeth. Teeko hopped onto the roof of a hut.

The warrior started yelling at the dog. The monkey screeched in laughter. Another warrior joined the chase. As the warrior ran by the hut, Teeko jumped on his back.

The monkey then hopped onto another roof. He turned and mocked the warrior. There was quite the commotion now as more warriors joined into the chase. Villagers came out of their huts to see what was happening.

Teddy's guard walked to the back of the hut to see what was happening. Hannah had hoped the guard would join in the chase, but he just stood at the back of the hut and laughed. Hopefully, he was distracted enough.

Hannah ran from the bushes. She ducked behind anything she could find as she made her way to the middle of the village. She glanced inside one of the huts. Inside was a bed with four tall bedposts. Lying on the bed was a woman who seemed very ill. The woman was covered by a colorful quilt. The bedroom looked so out of place in a village of grass huts.

Hannah was a little ashamed for getting distracted. Finally, she reached Teddy's hut. The guard had his back toward her. As quietly as possible she raised the latch. Inside she saw Teddy huddled in the corner. He was asleep.

Picking up a handful of pebbles, Hannah tossed them one at a time at the sleeping boy. Finally, he began to stir. Teddy yawned and stretched his arms. Then he saw the door was open.

"Hannah!" he yelled excitedly.

Hannah froze with fear. The guard turned around. He looked at Hannah and picked up his spear. She ran as fast as she could.

The guard latched the door and began to chase her. The warrior tossed his spear. It hit Hannah squarely in the back and she fell to the ground.

Chapter 15

The Beast of the Closet

Strangely, Hannah didn't feel any pain. She could feel the weight of the spear sticking out of her back. Then, she remembered the backpack. Hannah was grateful she hadn't tossed the carrots out when she got tired on the trail.

She was tempted to, but Hannah remembered the look on Joshua's face. He was serious about carrots. Now, she knew why. They had saved her life. Hannah slipped off the backpack and stood up.

The warrior had been smiling from a distance. Now, his expression turned to anger. Hannah pulled the spear out of the backpack. She slipped it back on. The warrior was coming at her.

Hannah picked up the spear. She jabbed it at the warrior. He seemed angry at first, and then he began to laugh. Hannah didn't really blame him. She realized how ridiculous it had to look.

She never dreamed she would get into a spear fight with a warrior. Even with the weapon she seemed overmatched. The warrior started moving in again. He was almost mocking her.

Hannah jabbed again. This time, the warrior was ready. He grabbed the spear. Hannah held the other end as tightly as possible.

The warrior started spinning in a circle. He was so big and strong that Hannah was lifted from her feet. She was flying as she clung to the end of the spear.

She was also getting very dizzy. Her grip loosened. Hannah went flying through the air. The warrior fell to the ground. He was too dizzy to tell where she had flown.

Hannah landed on the roof of a large hut. The thatched roof made for a soft landing. The leaves didn't hold up to the impact. Her legs slipped through first. Then she heard a cracking sound by her hands.

Her hands caught something stiff just below the roof. It felt like wire. She held on, but it dug into her hands. Hannah's fingers couldn't hold her much longer. She dropped to the ground.

It was dark inside the hut, except for the sunlight coming thought the new hole in the roof she had made. Hannah walked toward one of the walls. It was covered with wire, too. Suddenly, she realized where she was. Hannah had landed in the village closet, which was now the home of the beast of the forest.

Hannah heard a scuffling sound in the corner. Something very large was in the cage with her. She heard it in front of her. Then, she heard it in back of her. The beast moved around the edge of the cage. It seemed to be sizing her up. At first it moved slowly. Suddenly, it zipped to the other side of the building.

The sound came from behind her. To her right and then to her left the creature moved. She saw something round and white brush past the light.

It looked familiar. She wondered about something. Hannah slowly slipped off the backpack. She unzipped it and grabbed a handful of carrots. Hannah tossed them into the light.

The beast moved in. It nibbled at the carrots. Hannah grabbed another bunch and walked closer. She looked into the animal's soft eyes. The beast took them from her hands being very careful not to bite her.

Hannah reached out and petted the soft fur. She reached above her head and scratched behind its ears. The beast seemed to enjoy it. Hannah was amazed. The beast of the forest was the size of a horse.

A horse? That gave Hannah another idea. She felt along the walls of the cage in the darkness. Three walls were right up against the hut. There was a space in front of the fourth wall. That had to be the front of the cage.

"If you got trapped in here," Hannah spoke to the beast, "there must be a cage door big enough for you to fit through."

Hannah felt along the cage until she found the latch. She found a way to unhook it. The cage door swung open. Hannah made a trail of carrots out of the cage. The beast ate its way to freedom. Hannah wanted to do one more thing before leaving the hut.

She hugged the beast again. Hannah stood on her tiptoes and leaned into the beast's ears.

"Will you help me?"

The beast couldn't answer of course, but Hannah hoped the answer would have been yes. The beast lowered its head to the ground. It flexed its long ears forward. Hannah climbed up the nose of the beast and sat on its back.

"Hi Ho Hoppity!" Hannah shouted.

With that, the beast burst through the side of the hut. In the daylight, the villagers saw Hannah sitting on the back of the black and white beast. They ran in all directions in fear.

"You'd think they'd never seen a giant rabbit before," Hannah said to the beast in great delight.

The rabbit and Hannah seemed to communicate well. Whichever direction Hannah leaned, the rabbit would turn. They hopped to the hut in the center of the village.

"Snack time," said Hannah.

The rabbit bit the side of the hut off. Teddy cowered in the corner.

"Come on, Teddy!" shouted Hannah.

It was the first time Teddy had noticed Hannah on the back of the rabbit. He ran toward them. Hannah reached out and pulled him up. Away they hopped across the village.

Chief Honcho came out of his hut. "Stop them!" he shouted to his warriors.

The warriors stopped running away and started chasing Hannah and Teddy. Hannah shouted for the beast to stop when they reached the edge of the jungle. Teeko jumped from the roof of a hut onto the rabbit. Fuzzbundle crawled out from under a hut.

Spears flew around them. "Let's go," shouted Hannah.

The giant rabbit didn't react. The warriors were closing in.

"Giddy-up!" Hannah tried again. Still nothing.

Then she remembered, "Hi Ho Hoppity!"

The rabbit bolted into the jungle. The warriors were very close. The rabbit darted in and out of trees. Hannah turned back to see where the warriors were.

That was a mistake. When she looked forward again, the first thing she saw was a tree limb. It was too late to duck. Her arms caught the limb and suddenly she was swinging in the air.

The rabbit stopped. Teddy was trying to get it to go back. The warriors were closing fast. Hannah made a decision. It was too late for her.

"Hi Ho Hoppity," she yelled again. The rabbit bolted off into the jungle with Teddy and Teeko as the warriors surrounded her.

Chapter 16

Into the Daylight

No matter what he said, Teddy couldn't get the rabbit to stop. He wiped tears from his eyes as he thought about Hannah. The rabbit hopped on into the jungle. Fuzzbundle barked at its heels. He was trying to turn the rabbit around.

It was no use. The rabbit darted up the trail. Fuzzbundle was confused. He wanted to help both Hannah and Teddy. Finally, the dog turned back. He ran back to the tree that caught Hannah.

She was gone. The only thing left was the backpack. Fuzzbundle whined as he sniffed the bag. The dog caught a whiff that gave him an idea. Fuzzbundle clutched the bag and chased back after Teddy.

The dog caught up. The backpack had the rabbit's attention. Teddy saw what was happening.

"Good boy, Fuzzbundle! Let's turn this beast around."

But Fuzzbundle didn't turn the rabbit around. Instead the dog led the rabbit up the trail. Higher and higher they went up the side of the mountain. Fuzzbundle reached the spot of the avalanche.

At the top of the rock pile was a small hole. The dog dropped the backpack into the hole. It rolled down the steps. The giant rabbit stopped. It climbed to the top of the rock pile next to Fuzzbundle.

The rabbit started digging. Rocks and dirt were flying furiously behind the great beast. In a matter of minutes the stairway to the cave was cleared. The rabbit bounded down the stairs. Teddy ducked down to keep from bumping his head.

The rabbit burst through the door. The cave people peeked out of their huts. Teddy saw the little movements. He slipped off the back of the rabbit and stood upon the throne.

"It's me, Teddy. Come out. I have something important to say!"

The people timidly gathered at the bottom of the stairs in front of the throne. They were ready to run at the first sudden movement of the rabbit.

"Hannah is in trouble. She needs our help."

"Bring her to us. We would be glad to help her," someone shouted.

"That's not how it works," Teddy explained. "We have to go to her."

"Is she in the cave?" asked another.

"She's in the village," Teddy said.

Teeko jumped onto the back of the throne. He pointed up the stairway.

"We can't go outside. It's dangerous. Hannah is the Brave One, not us."

"We can all be brave," Teddy tried to explain. "Hannah didn't come to be brave for us. She came to teach us to be brave. I'm going back for her if I have to go alone."

Suddenly, carrots and coconuts fell from the hole in the roof. The rabbit caught sight of the carrots and bounded down the stairs. Teeko followed for the coconuts. The people scattered in all directions, diving behind rocks.

Teddy walked down the steps. "Why are you all hiding? What are you afraid of? Are you carrots or people? If you are a carrot, be afraid for the beast might eat you. If not, why are you afraid of my friend?"

"We must have courage! Now is the time!" Teddy was so angry he shouted. His voice rang off the walls of the cave.

A door to a hut in the back of the room opened. Out came Father Timekeeper. The big clock was around his neck. The thick book was under his arm. He shuffled past the pool of water. He stared at the rabbit and the monkey.

Father Timekeeper placed the book on the table. He thumbed through the pages. "Carry the three… Add the nine… He flipped through more pages. Giant carrot-eating beast…little monkey…I see, I see."

"It seems young Teddy is right," announced Father Timekeeper. "According to my calculations, it is time to have courage. The choice is yours, but time is running out."

Teddy looked around the cave. Whenever he caught the glimpse of anyone, they quickly ducked back behind their rocks. Sadly, Teddy turned and walked up the steps to the throne.

When he reached the top, he made one more plea. "This isn't a life. We sit in the darkness and quiver in fear. If we stand against the warriors, we may not make it, but what we fight for is worth it. I've been outside. It's both terrifying and beautiful. For too long I've been too afraid to really live. I've been too afraid of the unknown to learn anything new. In the short time I was outside, I did learn something new. I learned that having courage isn't a feeling, it's a choice. If you choose to have courage, you will have it!"

Teddy stepped through the door and started walking toward the daylight. Fuzzbundle barked twice. The giant rabbit and Teeko followed the dog up the steps.

Teddy was sad when he reached daylight. He felt they were running out of time. Suddenly there was another rumbling sound. Teddy and the animals raced for shelter behind a boulder. This time the avalanche was farther away. At first Teddy thought that was good news. Then he noticed that both pathways were wiped out.

He felt totally defeated. Just as he was about to give up hope, he heard something. Someone was coming up the stairway. It was Father Timekeeper. He was moving slowly.

"I'm with you son," said Father Timekeeper.

Teddy was encouraged by the support, but one feeble old man wasn't his idea of an army. Then, Teddy noticed someone behind the old man. In fact, there were several people behind Father Timekeeper.

One by one, all the people of the cave came forth. They gathered around Teddy. There were no pathways down the mountain after the avalanche.

"Now what do we do?" asked a child.

"Have courage!" said Teddy.

He ran and jumped off the cliff. The people gasped. Seconds of silence passed. Suddenly, Teddy bounced back into view.

"You never know what might happen. You might just soar!"

Teddy's courage was infectious. Soon, all the people of the caves had bounced to the bottom of the mountain. Finally, the giant rabbit jumped. Teeko clapped for joy when the beast finally came to rest on the trampoline. It was time to assemble the army.

Chapter 17

Freedom

Chief Honcho acted as the judge. Hannah sat silently. There wasn't much she could really say for herself. She was gagged.

"Does the defendant have anything to say for herself?" asked Chief Honcho.

Hannah made a muffled cry through the cloth. She struggled against the vines that tied her hands.

"No?" said Chief Honcho. "Then I find you guilty of destruction of property, aiding the enemy, and letting a really scary beast loose on the village. You are sentenced to the circle of death for each count against you."

"Captain, you may now remove the gag."

As soon as the cloth was removed Hannah started talking. "What kind of trial is this? I didn't even get a chance to defend myself."

"I asked you if you had anything to say. If you refuse to speak clearly, what should I do?" smiled the judge. "Now, captain, bring in the circles of death!"

It took courage for the cave people to jump off the cliff. It took courage to leave the cave. Very quickly, Teddy had transformed them into a fierce army. For too long they had been afraid. Bravery was a welcome change.

It was starting to get dark. That was fine with the people of the cave. They were used to darkness. Most of the villagers were in the meeting hut for the trial when Teddy arrived with his army.

A guard walked around the edge of the jungle keeping watch. Fuzzbundle walked up to the guard. The warrior pointed his spear at the dog. Fuzzbundle clinched it in his teeth and started tugging. He pulled to guard into the jungle.

Four cave people wrapped vines around him and placed a gag in his mouth. The scuffle drew the attention of another guard. The people slipped back into the jungle. The guard saw the bound warrior and bent down to help him. Father Timekeeper snuck up and bopped him on the head with his record book. The second guard was knocked out and ready to be tied.

Meanwhile, Teddy and Teeko had located Hannah in the meeting hut. Teeko climbed down from the roof to a window. Two spears were within reach. The monkey slowly lifted one out. He dropped it to Teddy.

Teddy passed it on to one of the cave people. The monkey grabbed the second one and dropped it to Teddy. He passed it along, too. They were about to move to another window when a hush fell over the crowd in the meeting hut.

Teddy could hear women muffling their crying. He could hear men letting out gasps of horror. Something terrible was happening, and it was most likely happening to Hannah. Teddy let out a loud whistle. All the cave people rushed to the meeting hut.

The giant rabbit gnawed off a wall of the hut. Teddy climbed into the room. Chief Honcho and the warriors were shocked. The chief looked at Teddy.

"Grab him!" the chief ordered his warriors.

Two warriors lunged at Teddy's feet. Two cave people grabbed his arms. Teddy was the rope in a tug-of-war. One of the warriors reached up to Teddy's pocket to get a better grip. The pocket tore open. The red and yellow ball bounced on the floor.

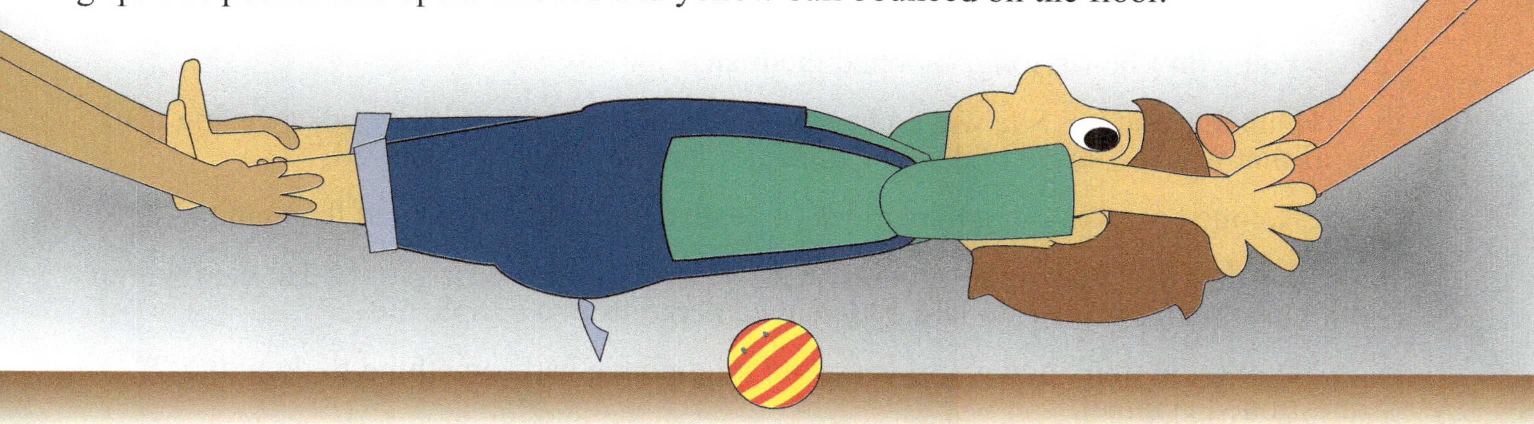

Everyone stopped. The people of the village bowed.

"Prince Theodore?" asked Chief Honcho.

A village woman ran from the hut. She came back leading a frail, but beautiful woman. Hannah recognized her as the woman who was asleep in the bed in the hut.

"Princess Millicent," whispered one of the cave people. "She's still alive."

The village woman led the princess to Teddy. Millicent reached out her hands and gently asked to see the red and yellow ball. Teddy handed it to her.

She looked it over carefully. Then she looked into Teddy's eyes.

"You look so much like your father," she said as a tear trickled down her face.

Teddy looked up at her, "Are you my mother?"

Millicent smiled, "Yes, my little prince."

Teddy hugged her. All the people (except the chief and the warriors) cheered.

"Long live Chief Theodore," someone shouted.

"Death to Chief Honcho," someone else shouted.

"Where did they go?" another asked.

Chief Honcho and the warriors were gone. They had slipped away during all the commotion and ran to the beach. The men had set sail in the chief's boat for another island. In the face of true courage, they had no other choice but to run for their lives.

Another woman started crying loudly. "Poor Hannah."

The joy faded from the crowd. One of the men fought back tears as he explained to Teddy and the cave dwellers that they were too late.

"Poor Hannah, she was so courageous to the very end. She faced the circles of death without a bit of fear. It was so inspiring."

Sobbing was heard throughout the crowd.

"I'm right here," said Hannah.

"You won't be for long," sobbed the man.

Hannah stood up. She waved her arms. "I'm okay. I don't know what the big deal is. If that was the circle of death, I'd like another serving. I'm starved."

"No one has ever eaten the circles of death and lived," explained the man.

"That's true," explained another. "Giroy Smove was the first to try. He died within minutes. Such a shame, to live 130 years and die from a simple meal."

"Don't you think being 130 years old might have had something to do with it?" questioned Hannah.

"Then there was Joval Cornbunk. He was only 20. He bit into the circle of death on a dare. We think he died almost instantly."

"You think he died almost instantly?" asked Hannah.

"There are conflicting reports. Some people thought they heard him scream as he fell from the coconut tree. That would indicate that he may have been alive before hitting the rocks below."

"Any chance that falling on rocks might have killed him?" asked Hannah.

"Hmm," a thoughtful sound came over the crowd.

Hannah smiled. She picked up another circle of death and bit into it. It was sweet and juicy.

"We call this pineapple where we come from. It's a delicious fruit. You should try it on solid ground while you're still young enough to enjoy it. If you do that, I think you'll be just fine."

Teddy hugged Hannah. Then, he took a slice of pineapple. He bit into it. The villagers held their breaths.

"It's delicious," said Teddy. "I think you could make a good cake out of something like this."

Chapter 18

The Rule of the Doors

Hannah rode on the back of the giant rabbit with Teddy and Teeko. They were at the head of the parade on the bright, sunny morning. The villagers followed along singing happy songs about courage and Hannah.

It was one of those happy-sad times for Hannah. She missed her mom and her normal life. Still, she was afraid once she left the island, she would never be able to come back. Deep down, she knew that even if she stayed, it wouldn't be the same. She had faced her fears and chose courage. Now, it was time to move on.

Soon they reached the beach. A tall, gray haired figure was walking at the edge of the water. Hannah was so happy Joshua had come to see her home. She slid from the rabbit and ran to meet him.

Joshua put his arm around her. "I am so proud of you. Look how far a little courage can take you." He gestured toward the villagers.

The group was spreading out on the beach. Everyone wanted to give Hannah a hug and thank her. She took time for them all.

Finally, she got to Teddy. A few days ago, he seemed like such a child. He had changed. The young prince was ready to take the throne. Hannah got on her knees and hugged Fuzzbundle.

"I love you, you silly mutt," she fought back the tears. Teeko hopped onto her back. The monkey gave her a warm hug. "You too, my little buddy."

That was almost everyone. A small boat was sailing up the coast. It was beautiful. The sunlight glinted off the pearl finish. As it drew closer, Hannah saw the white dolphins pulling it.

The boat gently glided to shore. Joshua greeted the passenger and extended his hand. An elegantly dressed woman carrying a white parasol stepped to the shore. Princess Millicent walked to Hannah. She looked so much stronger and happier today.

"Thank you for bringing my child home," she said. "You have made me so happy. I would like to give you something to show my appreciation."

She opened her purse. At first Hannah wanted to refuse. Then, she saw the object. Millicent held out the red and yellow ball.

"Teddy and I wanted you to have this."

Fuzzbundle barked.

Millicent laughed, "and Fuzzbundle."

Hannah took the ball and smiled. There was nothing more she had to say. She started to walk toward the closet.

"One warning," said Joshua. "When you open the door, be sure to step through. Once it's opened you can't change your mind. If the door closes and you don't step through, you can never use that door again."

"What?" Hannah panicked.

"It's the Rule of the Doors," said Joshua.

"Rule of the Doors? Why isn't that rule posted *on* the door?" cried Hannah.

She ran to the wall. Hannah found the doorknob. She turned it and pulled. Suddenly, the whole door turned to sand and fell to the beach.

Joshua walked up behind her. "I take it you've opened the door from this side before."

Hannah gulped back the tears. Her throat tightened. She nodded yes.

"I didn't know," she whimpered.

Millicent walked up to her. She pulled a lacy handkerchief from her purse. The princess handed it to Hannah.

"Now dry your eyes. All is not lost." She said as she pulled off one of her white gloves.

She stuck two fingers in her mouth and let off a whistle, just like Teddy. Millicent looked over the water and waved. The dolphins beat their fins on the water.

"I have been dying to ride that giant rabbit," said Millicent. "Why don't you borrow my boat? Our aquatic friends might have a solution to your problem."

Hannah got into the boat. Some of the villagers gave it a shove. It drifted away from the beach. The white dolphins tucked their noses into the loops of rope dangling in the water. Hannah looked back at the beach.

She waved until she was out of sight of the beach. The dolphins swiftly pulled the boat as Hannah drifted off to sleep. When she awoke, the boat had stopped. It was on a tiny island.

It wasn't exactly an island. It was only about six feet across. There was only one thing on the island. It was a door. Hannah stepped out of the boat. She studied the door.

One thing she knew for certain. Once she opened the door she was going to step through. Hannah had one concern. Which side of the door should she open? She started to walk around it.

"Ouch!" she smacked right into a wall on the right side of the door. She felt around the left side of the door. Although it appeared as if she could walk around the door she could not.

Satisfied that her only choice was the right choice, Hannah grasped the doorknob. It didn't turn to sand. That was a good sign. She turned the knob. She stepped through. She closed the door behind her. It was completely dark.

Hannah reached out her arms and stepped forward. Something brushed against her face. Instinctively she swatted at it. The string caught her hand. With a click the light came on.

"Don't worry, Sweety. The locksmith is here. We'll get you out."

Hannah smiled. It was her mother's voice. A clicking sound was followed by the door opening. Hannah's mother grabbed her and pulled her out of the pantry. They hugged.

"I'm fine mom," said Hannah.

"Trapped in the pantry for over an hour and you say you're fine?" asked Hannah's mom. "This can't be my little girl. When did you become the brave one?"

Hannah giggled.

Millie came into the kitchen. "I'm missing all the excitement."

The locksmith was picking up his tools. Millie picked up his business card. She read it and smiled.

"I don't think you're done yet," said aunt Millie. "I think the doorknob is loose on the other side. Can you tighten it?"

The locksmith stepped into the pantry with his tools. Millie closed the door.

"Is that a good idea?" asked Hannah's mom. "He could get trapped in there."

Hannah's mom turned the door knob and slowly opened the door, not wanting to bump the man. "I'm just checking to make sure you're not stuck."

Hannah's mom looked around the pantry. "He's not in here!"

Hannah's mom walked to the painting of the little door on the wall. She looked at it closely. She walked back out of the pantry and looked at Aunt Millie. "Wasn't that a painting of a closed door this morning? I don't remember the little beach with the boat pulled up on shore."

Just then a door slammed behind her. Hannah's mom turned around. She pointed at the wall. The painting now showed a closed door.

"That's just the way it was this morning," said Millie.

"Maybe I'm that one that needs to lie down," said Hannah's mom as she walked out of the kitchen.

Aunt Millie pulled the locksmith's business card out of her pocket. She handed it to Hannah. The card read: Alexander's Big Chief Lock Service.

"Teddy's dad?" asked Hannah.

"Has gone home," smiled Aunt Millie.

Made in the USA
Monee, IL
11 June 2023

35600422R00096